Toleration: A Very Short Introduction

VERY SHORT INTRODUCTIONS are for anyone wanting a stimulating and accessible way into a new subject. They are written by experts, and have been translated into more than 45 different languages.

The series began in 1995, and now covers a wide variety of topics in every discipline. The VSI library currently contains over 750 volumes—a Very Short Introduction to everything from Psychology and Philosophy of Science to American History and Relativity—and continues to grow in every subject area.

Very Short Introductions available now:

ABOLITIONISM Richard S. Newman
THE ABRAHAMIC RELIGIONS Charles L. Cohen
ACCOUNTING Christopher Nobes
ADDICTION Keith Humphreys
ADOLESCENCE Peter K. Smith
THEODOR W. ADORNO Andrew Bowie
ADVERTISING Winston Fletcher
AERIAL WARFARE Frank Ledwidge
AESTHETICS Bence Nanay
AFRICAN AMERICAN HISTORY Jonathan Scott Holloway
AFRICAN AMERICAN RELIGION Eddie S. Glaude Jr.
AFRICAN HISTORY John Parker and Richard Rathbone
AFRICAN POLITICS Ian Taylor
AFRICAN RELIGIONS Jacob K. Olupona
AGEING Nancy A. Pachana
AGNOSTICISM Robin Le Poidevin
AGRICULTURE Paul Brassley and Richard Soffe
ALEXANDER THE GREAT Hugh Bowden
ALGEBRA Peter M. Higgins
AMERICAN BUSINESS HISTORY Walter A. Friedman
AMERICAN CULTURAL HISTORY Eric Avila
AMERICAN FOREIGN RELATIONS Andrew Preston
AMERICAN HISTORY Paul S. Boyer
AMERICAN IMMIGRATION David A. Gerber
AMERICAN INTELLECTUAL HISTORY Jennifer Ratner-Rosenhagen
THE AMERICAN JUDICIAL SYSTEM Charles L. Zelden
AMERICAN LEGAL HISTORY G. Edward White
AMERICAN MILITARY HISTORY Joseph T. Glatthaar
AMERICAN NAVAL HISTORY Craig L. Symonds
AMERICAN POETRY David Caplan
AMERICAN POLITICAL HISTORY Donald Critchlow
AMERICAN POLITICAL PARTIES AND ELECTIONS L. Sandy Maisel
AMERICAN POLITICS Richard M. Valelly
THE AMERICAN PRESIDENCY Charles O. Jones
THE AMERICAN REVOLUTION Robert J. Allison
AMERICAN SLAVERY Heather Andrea Williams
THE AMERICAN SOUTH Charles Reagan Wilson
THE AMERICAN WEST Stephen Aron
AMERICAN WOMEN'S HISTORY Susan Ware
AMPHIBIANS T. S. Kemp
ANAESTHESIA Aidan O'Donnell
ANALYTIC PHILOSOPHY Michael Beaney

ANARCHISM Alex Prichard
ANCIENT ASSYRIA Karen Radner
ANCIENT EGYPT Ian Shaw
ANCIENT EGYPTIAN ART AND ARCHITECTURE Christina Riggs
ANCIENT GREECE Paul Cartledge
ANCIENT GREEK AND ROMAN SCIENCE Liba Taub
THE ANCIENT NEAR EAST Amanda H. Podany
ANCIENT PHILOSOPHY Julia Annas
ANCIENT WARFARE Harry Sidebottom
ANGELS David Albert Jones
ANGLICANISM Mark Chapman
THE ANGLO-SAXON AGE John Blair
ANIMAL BEHAVIOUR Tristram D. Wyatt
THE ANIMAL KINGDOM Peter Holland
ANIMAL RIGHTS David DeGrazia
ANSELM Thomas Williams
THE ANTARCTIC Klaus Dodds
ANTHROPOCENE Erle C. Ellis
ANTISEMITISM Steven Beller
ANXIETY Daniel Freeman and Jason Freeman
THE APOCRYPHAL GOSPELS Paul Foster
APPLIED MATHEMATICS Alain Goriely
THOMAS AQUINAS Fergus Kerr
ARBITRATION Thomas Schultz and Thomas Grant
ARCHAEOLOGY Paul Bahn
ARCHITECTURE Andrew Ballantyne
THE ARCTIC Klaus Dodds and Jamie Woodward
HANNAH ARENDT Dana Villa
ARISTOCRACY William Doyle
ARISTOTLE Jonathan Barnes
ART HISTORY Dana Arnold
ART THEORY Cynthia Freeland
ARTIFICIAL INTELLIGENCE Margaret A. Boden
ASIAN AMERICAN HISTORY Madeline Y. Hsu
ASTROBIOLOGY David C. Catling
ASTROPHYSICS James Binney
ATHEISM Julian Baggini
THE ATMOSPHERE Paul I. Palmer
AUGUSTINE Henry Chadwick
JANE AUSTEN Tom Keymer
AUSTRALIA Kenneth Morgan
AUTHORITARIANISM James Loxton
AUTISM Uta Frith
AUTOBIOGRAPHY Laura Marcus
THE AVANT GARDE David Cottington
THE AZTECS Davíd Carrasco
BABYLONIA Trevor Bryce
BACTERIA Sebastian G. B. Amyes
BANKING John Goddard and John O. S. Wilson
BARTHES Jonathan Culler
THE BEATS David Sterritt
BEAUTY Roger Scruton
LUDWIG VAN BEETHOVEN Mark Evan Bonds
BEHAVIOURAL ECONOMICS Michelle Baddeley
BESTSELLERS John Sutherland
THE BIBLE John Riches
BIBLICAL ARCHAEOLOGY Eric H. Cline
BIG DATA Dawn E. Holmes
BIOCHEMISTRY Mark Lorch
BIODIVERSITY CONSERVATION David Macdonald
BIOGEOGRAPHY Mark V. Lomolino
BIOGRAPHY Hermione Lee
BIOMETRICS Michael Fairhurst
ELIZABETH BISHOP Jonathan F. S. Post
BLACK HOLES Katherine Blundell
BLASPHEMY Yvonne Sherwood
BLOOD Chris Cooper
THE BLUES Elijah Wald
THE BODY Chris Shilling
THE BOHEMIANS David Weir
NIELS BOHR J. L. Heilbron
THE BOOK OF COMMON PRAYER Brian Cummings
THE BOOK OF MORMON Terryl Givens
BORDERS Alexander C. Diener and Joshua Hagen
THE BRAIN Michael O'Shea
BRANDING Robert Jones
THE BRICS Andrew F. Cooper
BRITISH ARCHITECTURE Dana Arnold
BRITISH CINEMA Charles Barr

THE BRITISH CONSTITUTION Martin Loughlin
THE BRITISH EMPIRE Ashley Jackson
BRITISH POLITICS Tony Wright
BUDDHA Michael Carrithers
BUDDHISM Damien Keown
BUDDHIST ETHICS Damien Keown
BYZANTIUM Peter Sarris
CALVINISM Jon Balserak
ALBERT CAMUS Oliver Gloag
CANADA Donald Wright
CANCER Nicholas James
CAPITALISM James Fulcher
CATHOLICISM Gerald O'Collins
THE CATHOLIC REFORMATION James E. Kelly
CAUSATION Stephen Mumford and Rani Lill Anjum
THE CELL Terence Allen and Graham Cowling
THE CELTS Barry Cunliffe
CHAOS Leonard Smith
GEOFFREY CHAUCER David Wallace
CHEMISTRY Peter Atkins
CHILD PSYCHOLOGY Usha Goswami
CHILDREN'S LITERATURE Kimberley Reynolds
CHINESE LITERATURE Sabina Knight
CHOICE THEORY Michael Allingham
CHRISTIAN ART Beth Williamson
CHRISTIAN ETHICS D. Stephen Long
CHRISTIANITY Linda Woodhead
CIRCADIAN RHYTHMS Russell Foster and Leon Kreitzman
CITIZENSHIP Richard Bellamy
CITY PLANNING Carl Abbott
CIVIL ENGINEERING David Muir Wood
THE CIVIL RIGHTS MOVEMENT Thomas C. Holt
CIVIL WARS Monica Duffy Toft
CLASSICAL LITERATURE William Allan
CLASSICAL MYTHOLOGY Helen Morales
CLASSICS Mary Beard and John Henderson
CLAUSEWITZ Michael Howard
CLIMATE Mark Maslin
CLIMATE CHANGE Mark Maslin
CLINICAL PSYCHOLOGY Susan Llewelyn and Katie Aafjes-van Doorn
COGNITIVE BEHAVIOURAL THERAPY Freda McManus
COGNITIVE NEUROSCIENCE Richard Passingham
THE COLD WAR Robert J. McMahon
COLONIAL AMERICA Alan Taylor
COLONIAL LATIN AMERICAN LITERATURE Rolena Adorno
COMBINATORICS Robin Wilson
COMEDY Matthew Bevis
COMMUNISM Leslie Holmes
COMPARATIVE LAW Sabrina Ragone and Guido Smorto
COMPARATIVE LITERATURE Ben Hutchinson
COMPETITION AND ANTITRUST LAW Ariel Ezrachi
COMPLEXITY John H. Holland
THE COMPUTER Darrel Ince
COMPUTER SCIENCE Subrata Dasgupta
CONCENTRATION CAMPS Dan Stone
CONDENSED MATTER PHYSICS Ross H. McKenzie
CONFUCIANISM Daniel K. Gardner
THE CONQUISTADORS Matthew Restall and Felipe Fernández-Armesto
CONSCIENCE Paul Strohm
CONSCIOUSNESS Susan Blackmore
CONTEMPORARY ART Julian Stallabrass
CONTEMPORARY FICTION Robert Eaglestone
CONTINENTAL PHILOSOPHY Simon Critchley
COPERNICUS Owen Gingerich
CORAL REEFS Charles Sheppard
CORPORATE SOCIAL RESPONSIBILITY Jeremy Moon
CORRUPTION Leslie Holmes
COSMOLOGY Peter Coles
COUNTRY MUSIC Richard Carlin
CREATIVITY Vlad Glăveanu
CRIME FICTION Richard Bradford
CRIMINAL JUSTICE Julian V. Roberts

CRIMINOLOGY Tim Newburn
CRITICAL THEORY Stephen Eric Bronner
THE CRUSADES Christopher Tyerman
CRYPTOGRAPHY Fred Piper and Sean Murphy
CRYSTALLOGRAPHY A. M. Glazer
THE CULTURAL REVOLUTION Richard Curt Kraus
DADA AND SURREALISM David Hopkins
DANTE Peter Hainsworth and David Robey
DARWIN Jonathan Howard
THE DEAD SEA SCROLLS Timothy H. Lim
DECADENCE David Weir
DECOLONIZATION Dane Kennedy
DEMENTIA Kathleen Taylor
DEMOCRACY Naomi Zack
DEMOGRAPHY Sarah Harper
DEPRESSION Jan Scott and Mary Jane Tacchi
DERRIDA Simon Glendinning
DESCARTES Tom Sorell
DESERTS Nick Middleton
DESIGN John Heskett
DEVELOPMENT Ian Goldin
DEVELOPMENTAL BIOLOGY Lewis Wolpert
THE DEVIL Darren Oldridge
DIASPORA Kevin Kenny
CHARLES DICKENS Jenny Hartley
DICTIONARIES Lynda Mugglestone
DINOSAURS David Norman
DIPLOMATIC HISTORY Joseph M. Siracusa
DOCUMENTARY FILM Patricia Aufderheide
DOSTOEVSKY Deborah Martinsen
DREAMING J. Allan Hobson
DRUGS Les Iversen
DRUIDS Barry Cunliffe
DYNASTY Jeroen Duindam
DYSLEXIA Margaret J. Snowling
EARLY MUSIC Thomas Forrest Kelly
THE EARTH Martin Redfern
EARTH SYSTEM SCIENCE Tim Lenton
ECOLOGY Jaboury Ghazoul
ECONOMICS Partha Dasgupta
EDUCATION Gary Thomas
EGYPTIAN MYTH Geraldine Pinch
EIGHTEENTH-CENTURY BRITAIN Paul Langford
ELECTIONS L. Sandy Maisel and Jennifer A. Yoder
THE ELEMENTS Philip Ball
EMOTION Dylan Evans
EMPIRE Stephen Howe
EMPLOYMENT LAW David Cabrelli
ENERGY SYSTEMS Nick Jenkins
ENGELS Terrell Carver
ENGINEERING David Blockley
THE ENGLISH LANGUAGE Simon Horobin
ENGLISH LITERATURE Jonathan Bate
THE ENLIGHTENMENT John Robertson
ENTREPRENEURSHIP Paul Westhead and Mike Wright
ENVIRONMENTAL ECONOMICS Stephen Smith
ENVIRONMENTAL ETHICS Robin Attfield
ENVIRONMENTAL LAW Elizabeth Fisher
ENVIRONMENTAL POLITICS Andrew Dobson
ENZYMES Paul Engel
THE EPIC Anthony Welch
EPICUREANISM Catherine Wilson
EPIDEMIOLOGY Rodolfo Saracci
ETHICS Simon Blackburn
ETHNOMUSICOLOGY Timothy Rice
THE ETRUSCANS Christopher Smith
EUGENICS Philippa Levine
THE EUROPEAN UNION Simon Usherwood and John Pinder
EUROPEAN UNION LAW Anthony Arnull
EVANGELICALISM John G. Stackhouse Jr.
EVIL Luke Russell
EVOLUTION Brian and Deborah Charlesworth
EXISTENTIALISM Thomas Flynn
EXPLORATION Stewart A. Weaver
EXTINCTION Paul B. Wignall
THE EYE Michael Land
FAIRY TALE Marina Warner

FAITH Roger Trigg
FAMILY LAW Jonathan Herring
MICHAEL FARADAY
Frank A. J. L. James
FASCISM Kevin Passmore
FASHION Rebecca Arnold
FEDERALISM Mark J. Rozell and
Clyde Wilcox
FEMINISM Margaret Walters
FEMINIST PHILOSOPHY
Katharine Jenkins
FILM Michael Wood
FILM MUSIC Kathryn Kalinak
FILM NOIR James Naremore
FIRE Andrew C. Scott
THE FIRST WORLD WAR
Michael Howard
FLUID MECHANICS Eric Lauga
FOLK MUSIC Mark Slobin
FOOD John Krebs
FORENSIC PSYCHOLOGY
David Canter
FORENSIC SCIENCE Jim Fraser
FORESTS Jaboury Ghazoul
FOSSILS Keith Thomson
FOUCAULT Gary Gutting
THE FOUNDING FATHERS
R. B. Bernstein
FRACTALS Kenneth Falconer
FREE SPEECH Nigel Warburton
FREE WILL Thomas Pink
FREEMASONRY Andreas Önnerfors
FRENCH CINEMA Dudley Andrew
FRENCH LITERATURE John D. Lyons
FRENCH PHILOSOPHY
Stephen Gaukroger and
Knox Peden
THE FRENCH REVOLUTION
William Doyle
FREUD Anthony Storr
FUNDAMENTALISM Malise Ruthven
FUNGI Nicholas P. Money
THE FUTURE Jennifer M. Gidley
GALAXIES John Gribbin
GALILEO Stillman Drake
GAME THEORY Ken Binmore
GANDHI Bhikhu Parekh
GARDEN HISTORY Gordon Campbell
GENDER HISTORY Antoinette Burton
GENES Jonathan Slack
GENIUS Andrew Robinson
GENOMICS John Archibald
GEOGRAPHY John Matthews and
David Herbert
GEOLOGY Jan Zalasiewicz
GEOMETRY Maciej Dunajski
GEOPHYSICAL AND
CLIMATE HAZARDS Bill McGuire
GEOPHYSICS William Lowrie
GEOPOLITICS Klaus Dodds
GERMAN LITERATURE
Nicholas Boyle
GERMAN PHILOSOPHY
Andrew Bowie
THE GHETTO Bryan Cheyette
GLACIATION David J. A. Evans
GLOBAL ECONOMIC HISTORY
Robert C. Allen
GLOBAL ISLAM Nile Green
GLOBALIZATION Manfred B. Steger
GOD John Bowker
GÖDEL'S THEOREM A. W. Moore
GOETHE Ritchie Robertson
THE GOTHIC Nick Groom
GOVERNANCE Mark Bevir
GRAVITY Timothy Clifton
THE GREAT DEPRESSION AND
THE NEW DEAL Eric Rauchway
THE GULAG Alan Barenberg
HABEAS CORPUS Amanda L. Tyler
HABERMAS James Gordon Finlayson
THE HABSBURG EMPIRE
Martyn Rady
HAPPINESS Daniel M. Haybron
THE HARLEM RENAISSANCE
Cheryl A. Wall
THE HEBREW BIBLE AS LITERATURE
Tod Linafelt
HEGEL Peter Singer
HEIDEGGER Michael Inwood
THE HELLENISTIC AGE
Peter Thonemann
HEREDITY John Waller
HERMENEUTICS Jens Zimmermann
HERODOTUS Jennifer T. Roberts
HIEROGLYPHS Penelope Wilson
HINDUISM Kim Knott
HISTORY John H. Arnold
THE HISTORY OF ASTRONOMY
Michael Hoskin

THE HISTORY OF CHEMISTRY
William H. Brock
THE HISTORY OF CHILDHOOD
James Marten
THE HISTORY OF CINEMA
Geoffrey Nowell-Smith
THE HISTORY OF COMPUTING
Doron Swade
THE HISTORY OF EMOTIONS
Thomas Dixon
THE HISTORY OF LIFE
Michael Benton
THE HISTORY OF MATHEMATICS
Jacqueline Stedall
THE HISTORY OF MEDICINE
William Bynum
THE HISTORY OF PHYSICS
J. L. Heilbron
THE HISTORY OF POLITICAL THOUGHT Richard Whatmore
THE HISTORY OF TIME
Leofranc Holford-Strevens
HIV AND AIDS Alan Whiteside
HOBBES Richard Tuck
HOLLYWOOD Peter Decherney
THE HOLY ROMAN EMPIRE
Joachim Whaley
HOME Michael Allen Fox
HOMER Barbara Graziosi
HORACE Llewelyn Morgan
HORMONES Martin Luck
HORROR Darryl Jones
HUMAN ANATOMY
Leslie Klenerman
HUMAN EVOLUTION Bernard Wood
HUMAN PHYSIOLOGY
Jamie A. Davies
HUMAN RESOURCE MANAGEMENT Adrian Wilkinson
HUMAN RIGHTS Andrew Clapham
HUMANISM Stephen Law
HUME James A. Harris
HUMOUR Noël Carroll
IBN SĪNĀ (AVICENNA)
Peter Adamson
THE ICE AGE Jamie Woodward
IDENTITY Florian Coulmas
IDEOLOGY Michael Freeden
IMAGINATION
Jennifer Gosetti-Ferencei
THE IMMUNE SYSTEM
Paul Klenerman
INDIAN CINEMA
Ashish Rajadhyaksha
INDIAN PHILOSOPHY Sue Hamilton
THE INDUSTRIAL REVOLUTION
Robert C. Allen
INFECTIOUS DISEASE Marta L. Wayne and Benjamin M. Bolker
INFINITY Ian Stewart
INFORMATION Luciano Floridi
INNOVATION Mark Dodgson and David Gann
INTELLECTUAL PROPERTY
Siva Vaidhyanathan
INTELLIGENCE Ian J. Deary
INTERNATIONAL LAW
Vaughan Lowe
INTERNATIONAL MIGRATION
Khalid Koser
INTERNATIONAL RELATIONS
Christian Reus-Smit
INTERNATIONAL SECURITY
Christopher S. Browning
INSECTS Simon Leather
INVASIVE SPECIES Julie Lockwood and Dustin Welbourne
IRAN Ali M. Ansari
ISLAM Malise Ruthven
ISLAMIC HISTORY Adam Silverstein
ISLAMIC LAW Mashood A. Baderin
ISOTOPES Rob Ellam
ITALIAN LITERATURE
Peter Hainsworth and David Robey
HENRY JAMES Susan L. Mizruchi
JAPANESE LITERATURE Alan Tansman
JESUS Richard Bauckham
JEWISH HISTORY David N. Myers
JEWISH LITERATURE Ilan Stavans
JOURNALISM Ian Hargreaves
JAMES JOYCE Colin MacCabe
JUDAISM Norman Solomon
JUNG Anthony Stevens
THE JURY Renée Lettow Lerner
KABBALAH Joseph Dan
KAFKA Ritchie Robertson
KANT Roger Scruton
KEYNES Robert Skidelsky
KIERKEGAARD Patrick Gardiner
KNOWLEDGE Jennifer Nagel

THE KORAN Michael Cook
KOREA Michael J. Seth
LAKES Warwick F. Vincent
LANDSCAPE ARCHITECTURE Ian H. Thompson
LANDSCAPES AND GEOMORPHOLOGY Andrew Goudie and Heather Viles
LANGUAGES Stephen R. Anderson
LATE ANTIQUITY Gillian Clark
LAW Raymond Wacks
THE LAWS OF THERMODYNAMICS Peter Atkins
LEADERSHIP Keith Grint
LEARNING Mark Haselgrove
LEIBNIZ Maria Rosa Antognazza
C. S. LEWIS James Como
LIBERALISM Michael Freeden
LIGHT Ian Walmsley
LINCOLN Allen C. Guelzo
LINGUISTICS Peter Matthews
LITERARY THEORY Jonathan Culler
LOCKE John Dunn
LOGIC Graham Priest
LOVE Ronald de Sousa
MARTIN LUTHER Scott H. Hendrix
MACHIAVELLI Quentin Skinner
MADNESS Andrew Scull
MAGIC Owen Davies
MAGNA CARTA Nicholas Vincent
MAGNETISM Stephen Blundell
MALTHUS Donald Winch
MAMMALS T. S. Kemp
MANAGEMENT John Hendry
NELSON MANDELA Elleke Boehmer
MAO Delia Davin
MARINE BIOLOGY Philip V. Mladenov
MARKETING Kenneth Le Meunier-FitzHugh
THE MARQUIS DE SADE John Phillips
MARTYRDOM Jolyon Mitchell
MARX Peter Singer
MATERIALS Christopher Hall
MATHEMATICAL ANALYSIS Richard Earl
MATHEMATICAL FINANCE Mark H. A. Davis
MATHEMATICS Timothy Gowers
MATTER Geoff Cottrell
THE MAYA Matthew Restall and Amara Solari
MEANING Emma Borg and Sarah A. Fisher
THE MEANING OF LIFE Terry Eagleton
MEASUREMENT David Hand
MEDICAL ETHICS Michael Dunn and Tony Hope
MEDICAL LAW Charles Foster
MEDIEVAL BRITAIN John Gillingham and Ralph A. Griffiths
MEDIEVAL LITERATURE Elaine Treharne
MEDIEVAL PHILOSOPHY John Marenbon
MEMORY Jonathan K. Foster
METAPHYSICS Stephen Mumford
METHODISM William J. Abraham
THE MEXICAN REVOLUTION Alan Knight
MICROBIOLOGY Nicholas P. Money
MICROBIOMES Angela E. Douglas
MICROECONOMICS Avinash Dixit
MICROSCOPY Terence Allen
THE MIDDLE AGES Miri Rubin
MILITARY JUSTICE Eugene R. Fidell
MILITARY STRATEGY Antulio J. Echevarria II
JOHN STUART MILL Gregory Claeys
MINERALS David Vaughan
MIRACLES Yujin Nagasawa
MODERN ARCHITECTURE Adam Sharr
MODERN ART David Cottington
MODERN BRAZIL Anthony W. Pereira
MODERN CHINA Rana Mitter
MODERN DRAMA Kirsten E. Shepherd-Barr
MODERN FRANCE Vanessa R. Schwartz
MODERN INDIA Craig Jeffrey
MODERN IRELAND Senia Pašeta
MODERN ITALY Anna Cento Bull
MODERN JAPAN Christopher Goto-Jones
MODERN LATIN AMERICAN LITERATURE Roberto González Echevarría
MODERN WAR Richard English

MODERNISM Christopher Butler
MOLECULAR BIOLOGY Aysha Divan and Janice A. Royds
MOLECULES Philip Ball
MONASTICISM Stephen J. Davis
THE MONGOLS Morris Rossabi
MONTAIGNE William M. Hamlin
MOONS David A. Rothery
MORMONISM Richard Lyman Bushman
MOUNTAINS Martin F. Price
MUHAMMAD Jonathan A. C. Brown
MULTICULTURALISM Ali Rattansi
MULTILINGUALISM John C. Maher
MUSIC Nicholas Cook
MUSIC AND TECHNOLOGY Mark Katz
MYTH Robert A. Segal
NANOTECHNOLOGY Philip Moriarty
NAPOLEON David A. Bell
THE NAPOLEONIC WARS Mike Rapport
NATIONALISM Steven Grosby
NATIVE AMERICAN LITERATURE Sean Teuton
NAVIGATION Jim Bennett
NAZI GERMANY Jane Caplan
NEGOTIATION Carrie Menkel-Meadow
NEOLIBERALISM Manfred B. Steger and Ravi K. Roy
NETWORKS Guido Caldarelli and Michele Catanzaro
THE NEW TESTAMENT Luke Timothy Johnson
THE NEW TESTAMENT AS LITERATURE Kyle Keefer
NEWTON Robert Iliffe
NIETZSCHE Michael Tanner
NINETEENTH-CENTURY BRITAIN Christopher Harvie and H. C. G. Matthew
THE NORMAN CONQUEST George Garnett
NORTH AMERICAN INDIANS Theda Perdue and Michael D. Green
NORTHERN IRELAND Marc Mulholland
NOTHING Frank Close
NUCLEAR PHYSICS Frank Close
NUCLEAR POWER Maxwell Irvine
NUCLEAR WEAPONS Joseph M. Siracusa
NUMBER THEORY Robin Wilson
NUMBERS Peter M. Higgins
NUTRITION David A. Bender
OBJECTIVITY Stephen Gaukroger
OBSERVATIONAL ASTRONOMY Geoff Cottrell
OCEANS Dorrik Stow
THE OLD TESTAMENT Michael D. Coogan
THE ORCHESTRA D. Kern Holoman
ORGANIC CHEMISTRY Graham Patrick
ORGANIZATIONS Mary Jo Hatch
ORGANIZED CRIME Georgios A. Antonopoulos and Georgios Papanicolaou
ORTHODOX CHRISTIANITY A. Edward Siecienski
OVID Llewelyn Morgan
PAGANISM Owen Davies
PAKISTAN Pippa Virdee
THE PALESTINIAN-ISRAELI CONFLICT Martin Bunton
PANDEMICS Christian W. McMillen
PARTICLE PHYSICS Frank Close
PAUL E. P. Sanders
IVAN PAVLOV Daniel P. Todes
PEACE Oliver P. Richmond
PENTECOSTALISM William K. Kay
PERCEPTION Brian Rogers
THE PERIODIC TABLE Eric R. Scerri
PHILOSOPHICAL METHOD Timothy Williamson
PHILOSOPHY Edward Craig
PHILOSOPHY IN THE ISLAMIC WORLD Peter Adamson
PHILOSOPHY OF BIOLOGY Samir Okasha
PHILOSOPHY OF LAW Raymond Wacks
PHILOSOPHY OF MIND Barbara Gail Montero
PHILOSOPHY OF PHYSICS David Wallace
PHILOSOPHY OF SCIENCE Samir Okasha
PHILOSOPHY OF RELIGION Tim Bayne

PHOTOGRAPHY Steve Edwards
PHYSICAL CHEMISTRY Peter Atkins
PHYSICS Sidney Perkowitz
PILGRIMAGE Ian Reader
PLAGUE Paul Slack
PLANETARY SYSTEMS Raymond T. Pierrehumbert
PLANETS David A. Rothery
PLANTS Timothy Walker
PLATE TECTONICS Peter Molnar
SYLVIA PLATH Heather Clark
PLATO Julia Annas
POETRY Bernard O'Donoghue
POLITICAL PHILOSOPHY David Miller
POLITICS Kenneth Minogue
POLYGAMY Sarah M. S. Pearsall
POPULISM Cas Mudde and Cristóbal Rovira Kaltwasser
POSTCOLONIALISM Robert J. C. Young
POSTMODERNISM Christopher Butler
POSTSTRUCTURALISM Catherine Belsey
POVERTY Philip N. Jefferson
PREHISTORY Chris Gosden
PRESOCRATIC PHILOSOPHY Catherine Osborne
PRIVACY Raymond Wacks
PROBABILITY John Haigh
PROGRESSIVISM Walter Nugent
PROHIBITION W. J. Rorabaugh
PROJECTS Andrew Davies
PROTESTANTISM Mark A. Noll
MARCEL PROUST Joshua Landy
PSEUDOSCIENCE Michael D. Gordin
PSYCHIATRY Tom Burns
PSYCHOANALYSIS Daniel Pick
PSYCHOLOGY Gillian Butler and Freda McManus
PSYCHOLOGY OF MUSIC Elizabeth Hellmuth Margulis
PSYCHOPATHY Essi Viding
PSYCHOTHERAPY Tom Burns and Eva Burns-Lundgren
PUBLIC ADMINISTRATION Stella Z. Theodoulou and Ravi K. Roy
PUBLIC HEALTH Virginia Berridge
PURITANISM Francis J. Bremer
THE QUAKERS Pink Dandelion
QUANTUM THEORY John Polkinghorne
RACISM Ali Rattansi
RADIOACTIVITY Claudio Tuniz
RASTAFARI Ennis B. Edmonds
READING Belinda Jack
THE REAGAN REVOLUTION Gil Troy
REALITY Jan Westerhoff
RECONSTRUCTION Allen C. Guelzo
THE REFORMATION Peter Marshall
REFUGEES Gil Loescher
RELATIVITY Russell Stannard
RELIGION Thomas A. Tweed
RELIGION IN AMERICA Timothy Beal
THE RENAISSANCE Jerry Brotton
RENAISSANCE ART Geraldine A. Johnson
RENEWABLE ENERGY Nick Jelley
REPTILES T. S. Kemp
REVOLUTIONS Jack A. Goldstone
RHETORIC Richard Toye
RISK Baruch Fischhoff and John Kadvany
RITUAL Barry Stephenson
RIVERS Nick Middleton
ROBOTICS Alan Winfield
ROCKS Jan Zalasiewicz
ROMAN BRITAIN Peter Salway
THE ROMAN EMPIRE Christopher Kelly
THE ROMAN REPUBLIC David M. Gwynn
ROMANTICISM Michael Ferber
ROUSSEAU Robert Wokler
THE RULE OF LAW Aziz Z. Huq
RUSSELL A. C. Grayling
THE RUSSIAN ECONOMY Richard Connolly
RUSSIAN HISTORY Geoffrey Hosking
RUSSIAN LITERATURE Catriona Kelly
RUSSIAN POLITICS Brian D. Taylor
THE RUSSIAN REVOLUTION S. A. Smith
SAINTS Simon Yarrow
SAMURAI Michael Wert
SAVANNAS Peter A. Furley
SCEPTICISM Duncan Pritchard
SCHIZOPHRENIA Chris Frith and Eve Johnstone
SCHOPENHAUER Christopher Janaway

SCIENCE AND RELIGION Thomas Dixon and Adam R. Shapiro
SCIENCE FICTION David Seed
THE SCIENTIFIC REVOLUTION Lawrence M. Principe
SCOTLAND Rab Houston
SECULARISM Andrew Copson
THE SELF Marya Schechtman
SEXUAL SELECTION Marlene Zuk and Leigh W. Simmons
SEXUALITY Véronique Mottier
WILLIAM SHAKESPEARE Stanley Wells
SHAKESPEARE'S COMEDIES Bart van Es
SHAKESPEARE'S SONNETS AND POEMS Jonathan F. S. Post
SHAKESPEARE'S TRAGEDIES Stanley Wells
GEORGE BERNARD SHAW Christopher Wixson
MARY SHELLEY Charlotte Gordon
THE SHORT STORY Andrew Kahn
SIKHISM Eleanor Nesbitt
SILENT FILM Donna Kornhaber
THE SILK ROAD James A. Millward
SLANG Jonathon Green
SLEEP Steven W. Lockley and Russell G. Foster
SMELL Matthew Cobb
ADAM SMITH Christopher J. Berry
SOCIAL AND CULTURAL ANTHROPOLOGY John Monaghan and Peter Just
SOCIALISM Michael Newman
SOCIAL PSYCHOLOGY Richard J. Crisp
SOCIAL SCIENCE Alexander Betts
SOCIAL WORK Sally Holland and Jonathan Scourfield
SOCIOLINGUISTICS John Edwards
SOCIOLOGY Steve Bruce
SOCRATES C. C. W. Taylor
SOFT MATTER Tom McLeish
SOPHOCLES Edith Hall
SOUND Mike Goldsmith
SOUTHEAST ASIA James R. Rush
THE SOVIET UNION Stephen Lovell
THE SPANISH CIVIL WAR Helen Graham
SPANISH LITERATURE Jo Labanyi
THE SPARTANS Andrew J. Bayliss
SPINOZA Roger Scruton
SPIRITUALITY Philip Sheldrake
SPORT Mike Cronin
STARS Andrew King
STATISTICS David J. Hand
STEM CELLS Jonathan Slack
STOICISM Brad Inwood
STRUCTURAL ENGINEERING David Blockley
STUART BRITAIN John Morrill
SUBURBS Carl Abbott
THE SUN Philip Judge
SUPERCONDUCTIVITY Stephen Blundell
SUPERSTITION Stuart Vyse
SURVEILLANCE David Lyon
SUSTAINABILITY Saleem Ali
SYMBIOSIS Nancy A. Moran
SYMMETRY Ian Stewart
SYNAESTHESIA Julia Simner
SYNTHETIC BIOLOGY Jamie A. Davies
SYSTEMS BIOLOGY Eberhard O. Voit
TAXATION Stephen Smith
TEETH Peter S. Ungar
TERRORISM Charles Townshend
THEATRE Marvin Carlson
THEOLOGY David F. Ford
THINKING AND REASONING Jonathan St B. T. Evans
THOUGHT Tim Bayne
THUCYDIDES Jennifer T. Roberts
TIBETAN BUDDHISM Matthew T. Kapstein
TIDES David George Bowers and Emyr Martyn Roberts
TIME Jenann Ismael
TOCQUEVILLE Harvey C. Mansfield
TOLERATION Andrew R. Murphy
J. R. R. TOLKIEN Matthew Townend
LEO TOLSTOY Liza Knapp
TOPOLOGY Richard Earl
TRAGEDY Adrian Poole
TRANSLATION Matthew Reynolds
THE TREATY OF VERSAILLES Michael S. Neiberg
TRIGONOMETRY Glen Van Brummelen
THE TROJAN WAR Eric H. Cline
ANTHONY TROLLOPE Dinah Birch
TRUST Katherine Hawley

THE TUDORS John Guy
TWENTIETH-CENTURY BRITAIN
Kenneth O. Morgan
TYPOGRAPHY Paul Luna
THE UNITED NATIONS
Jussi M. Hanhimäki
UNIVERSITIES AND COLLEGES
David Palfreyman and Paul Temple
THE U.S. CIVIL WAR Louis P. Masur
THE U.S. CONGRESS Donald A. Ritchie
THE U.S. CONSTITUTION
David J. Bodenhamer
THE U.S. SUPREME COURT
Linda Greenhouse
UTILITARIANISM
Katarzyna de Lazari-Radek and
Peter Singer
UTOPIANISM Lyman Tower Sargent
VATICAN II Shaun Blanchard and
Stephen Bullivant
VETERINARY SCIENCE James Yeates
THE VICTORIANS Martin Hewitt
THE VIKINGS Julian D. Richards
VIOLENCE Philip Dwyer
THE VIRGIN MARY
Mary Joan Winn Leith
THE VIRTUES Craig A. Boyd and
Kevin Timpe
VIRUSES Dorothy H. Crawford
VOLCANOES Michael J. Branney and
Jan Zalasiewicz
VOLTAIRE Nicholas Cronk
WAR AND RELIGION Jolyon Mitchell
and Joshua Rey
WAR AND TECHNOLOGY
Alex Roland
WATER John Finney
WAVES Mike Goldsmith
WEATHER Storm Dunlop
SIMONE WEIL
A. Rebecca Rozelle-Stone
THE WELFARE STATE David Garland
WITCHCRAFT Malcolm Gaskill
WITTGENSTEIN A. C. Grayling
WORK Stephen Fineman
WORLD MUSIC Philip Bohlman
WORLD MYTHOLOGY
David Leeming
THE WORLD TRADE
ORGANIZATION
Amrita Narlikar
WORLD WAR II Gerhard L. Weinberg
WRITING AND SCRIPT
Andrew Robinson
ZIONISM Michael Stanislawski
ÉMILE ZOLA Brian Nelson

Available soon:

PSYCHOLINGUISTICS
Ferenda Ferreria

ANTHONY TROLLOPE
Dinah Birch

Andrew R. Murphy

TOLERATION

A Very Short Introduction

OXFORD
UNIVERSITY PRESS

Oxford University Press is a department of the University of Oxford. It furthers the University's objective of excellence in research, scholarship, and education by publishing worldwide. Oxford is a registered trade mark of Oxford University Press in the UK and in certain other countries.

Published in the United States of America by Oxford University Press
198 Madison Avenue, New York, NY 10016, United States of America.

Library of Congress Cataloging-in-Publication Data
Names: Murphy, Andrew R., 1967– author.
Title: Toleration : a very short introduction / Andrew R. Murphy.
Description: New York, NY : Oxford University Press, [2025] | Series: Very short introductions
Identifiers: LCCN 2024024862 (print) | LCCN 2024024863 (ebook) | ISBN 9780197664957 (paperback) | ISBN 9780197664971 (epub)
Subjects: LCSH: Toleration.
Classification: LCC HM1271.M868 2025 (print) | LCC HM1271 (ebook) | DDC 179/.9—dc23/eng/20240812
LC record available at https://lccn.loc.gov/2024024862
LC ebook record available at https://lccn.loc.gov/2024024863

Integrated Books International, United States of America

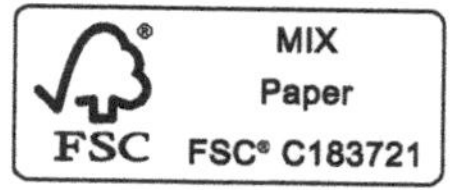

Contents

Acknowledgments

Having learned so much from so many *Very Short Introductions* over the years, I am deeply honored for a volume of mine to join the series. This book represents the culmination of more than thirty years spent exploring toleration in its many forms, across a number of different historical contexts. Over that span of time, I have benefited from conversations with countless colleagues (many of them experts in their own right). It's impossible to name them all—indeed, it's impossible to remember them all!—but I must single out Teresa Bejan, Jane Calvert, John Coffey, Mark Goldie, David Gutterman, Evan Haefeli, John Smolenski, Scott Sowerby, and Adrian Weimer. I am deeply grateful to these colleagues, interlocutors, and friends for the role they have played in my own ongoing education on the topic of toleration. Whatever virtues this manuscript might possess stem in large part from their influence.

I remain indebted, too, to students and colleagues at each of the universities that I have been fortunate enough to call home (Villanova, Chicago, Valparaiso, Rutgers, Virginia Commonwealth, and Michigan) and to audiences at conferences, symposia, and workshops too numerous to mention over the years. Most recently, thanks are particularly due to Ekaterina Olson Shipyatsky, who read several versions of this manuscript with a fresh set of eyes and offered valuable stylistic and substantive feedback.

I have been working with Oxford University Press for nearly twenty years now and continue to benefit from the professionalism and good cheer of everyone there. This is my second book under the editorial guidance of Nancy Toff, who not only helped enormously with the volume's conceptualization (drawing on her deep knowledge of the *Very Short Introduction* series), but also recruited two outstanding reviewers whose detailed feedback on my original proposal, as well as a later draft of the entire manuscript, led to profound improvements in the final product. Nancy wields her editorial pen like a scalpel, with (I like to think) equally healthful results. Meredith Taylor, who came on board as project editor as the book made its way through the publication process, handled every detail and request with grace and care. Working with OUP continues to be a delight.

Finally, it goes without saying—but I'll say it anyway—that none of this would have been possible without Beth, Sam, Pete, and Lilli.

List of illustrations

Chapter 1
Introducing toleration

"It is now no more that toleration is spoken of," President George Washington wrote to the Hebrew Congregation in Newport, Rhode Island, in 1790, "as if it was by the indulgence of one class of people, that another enjoyed the exercise of their inherent natural rights." Despite Washington's confident assertion that the young nation had moved beyond toleration, however—to say nothing of the countless Americans who, even as he wrote, had yet to enjoy "the exercise of their inherent natural rights"—toleration *is* still "spoken of." Celebrated by some, excoriated by others; praised as a noble aspiration in some settings, lamented as a half-hearted half-measure in others—toleration continues to evoke roughly equal parts admiration and condemnation in a polarized world riven by religious discord and cultural conflict. Depending on one's perspective, it represents a cardinal achievement of modern political regimes, a grudging and insufficient measure of civil respect, or a set of practices hopelessly tainted by their association with imperialism, colonialism, and Eurocentrism. Or, perhaps, a bit of all three.

Rooted in the Latin *tolerare*—to bear with, or endure, or allow—toleration remains one of the most foundational, and contentious, concepts in contemporary political discourse. Its modern origins lie in the realm of religion, where the most

To the Hebrew Congregation in Newport
Rhode Island.

Gentlemen.

While I receive, with much satisfaction, your Address replete with expressions of affection and esteem; I rejoice in the opportunity of assuring you, that I shall always retain a grateful remembrance of the cordial welcome I experienced in my visit to Newport, from all classes of Citizens.

The reflection on the days of difficulty and danger which are past is rendered the more sweet, from a consciousness that they are succeeded by days of uncommon prosperity and security. If we have wisdom to make the best use of the advantages with which we are now favored, we cannot fail, under the just administration of a good Government, to become a great and a happy people.

The Citizens of the United States of America have a right to applaud themselves for having given to mankind examples of an enlarged and liberal policy: a policy worthy of imitation. All possess alike liberty of conscience and immunities of citizenship. It is now no more that toleration is spoken of, as if it was by the indulgence of one class of people, that another enjoyed the exercise of their inherent natural rights. For happily the

1. In a 1790 letter to the Hebrew Congregation in Newport, Rhode Island, George Washington wrote, "It is now no more that toleration is spoken of, as if it was by the indulgence of one class of people, that another enjoyed the exercise of their inherent natural rights."

influential arguments in its favor emerged during the sixteenth and seventeenth centuries, and where calls for toleration responded to the presence of multiple competing religious communities in the wake of the Protestant Reformation. Over the intervening years, theorists and activists have invoked toleration in an ever-wider range of political debates. Today, toleration is routinely invoked—again, at times to be praised as a hard-won political achievement, at others to be denounced as a woefully inadequate compromise—in contemporary disputes involving race, gender, religion, ethnicity, sexuality, free speech, and civil liberties.

As a political term, toleration refers to the guarantee of political or legal protections to members of groups facing hostility or disapproval from their neighbors or the state (or both). Questions of toleration arise wherever individuals or groups face hostile social environments and stand in need of such protection. Toleration thus only becomes an issue in certain times and places, in situations of conflict between groups (religious, cultural, ethnic, sexual, and so on) or between such groups and their governments. In practice, there is not one fixed thing called "toleration"; rather varieties of toleration are shaped by the political, religious, historical, and social contexts in which they appear. (Some commentators have also used the term "toleration" to identify a personal virtue, denoting an individual willingness to allow things of which one disapproves. Although the two senses are related, the focus here is primarily on toleration's social and political dimensions.)

Historically, this political term emerged, in its modern form at least, from the debates over religion that shook sixteenth- and seventeenth-century Europe, and thus toleration has always appeared as part of conflicts between competing religious groups. Although it represents a considerable improvement over persecution for those in need of its protections, toleration nonetheless pales when compared to fuller understandings of liberty, such as religious freedom or (even more expansively) liberty of conscience. This tension between toleration as a minimal protection of basic rights and the aspirational nature of claims to freedom and equality, evident in George Washington's message to the Hebrew Congregation of Newport, will play a significant role in this account of toleration's history and future prospects.

Since the early modern period, phenomena such as globalization, colonialism, imperialism, and increasingly widespread migration have brought the circumstances of toleration to the fore in particularly profound ways. However, the condition of diverse groups facing the challenges of coexistence within a single political territory is hardly unique to modern times. As both an idea and a contested political practice, toleration's conceptual foundations have developed over time, shaped by both philosophical arguments advanced in its favor (as well as arguments against it, offered by critics) and the concrete actions of rulers and regimes who have attempted to implement it as a way of dealing with various types of difference. As an inheritance from past struggles, toleration still has an important role to play in a globalized, increasingly connected, highly polarized, and ever more diverse world.

Three challenges

Writing about toleration poses three important challenges; addressing each is essential to understanding this complex phenomenon. First, the concept itself can seem counter-intuitive, since it involves a complex and simultaneous blend of rejection and acceptance. Toleration combines rejection or disapproval—of particular individuals, groups, beliefs, and practices—on the one hand with legal and political acceptance of those groups on the other. In other words, it offers an end to punishment or persecution without necessarily offering approval or endorsement. But despite the hopes of many of its supporters or the critiques of many of its detractors, toleration always comes with limits; not everything is tolerated. In debating what should be tolerated, and why, participants in toleration debates also, simultaneously, address what should not be tolerated, and why not. Governments (or, more accurately, their designated agents or other public officials) adopt tolerationist policies, or choose not to, for a complex blend of reasons, from the principled to the pragmatic.

Reflecting this somewhat counterintuitive nature of toleration, Rainer Forst, one of the foremost contemporary analysts of the topic, has insisted that its essence lies in the noninterference with practices or beliefs that one considers wrong, illustrating the competing impulses and judgments inherent in the concept and its associated practices. Condemnation sits, uneasily at times, alongside permission. As such, toleration often falls short of ideals like respect and affirmation, which has led some observers to offer a less-than-rousing endorsement, as when the philosopher Ramchandra Gandhi gave tolerance only "two cheers," positioning it somewhere better than mere coexistence or outright conflict but well short of love and compassion as a response to difference.

Gandhi's "two cheers" comment provides a nice segue into the second challenging aspect of writing about toleration: In the English language at least, toleration is shadowed by a close cognate term—*tolerance*–that has its own conceptual history and range of meanings. Thus, toleration is frequently associated with, though distinct from, a purportedly related individual virtue of tolerance. But there is little consensus on the meaning of tolerance, and even less on the nature of its relationship to toleration. Many who write about the subject assume that practices of toleration must necessarily be undergirded by, or flow out of, a personal disposition, or virtue, of tolerance; that is, they assume that a certain type of person (a tolerant one) is most likely to support and enact certain types of political or legal policies (toleration).

This presumption of a necessary relationship between personal qualities and political outcomes, however, has proven controversial, and counter-examples abound. Intolerant groups—those who judge the beliefs and practices of others harshly, or condemn those who believe or behave in ways they find mistaken or repugnant—have frequently supported robust notions of toleration. One such individual, a key figure in the history of toleration, was Roger Williams: predestinarian Calvinist, English Separatist, founder of Rhode Island, and ardent defender of liberty of conscience. Conversely, many whom we would likely call tolerant, who refrain from directing harsh criticisms at those with whom they differ, have often endorsed the restriction of rights for those they deem a threat to public order; witness the widespread popularity of the Patriot Act in the wake of the September 11 attacks (or, to take a historical example, Thomas Hobbes's deep concern about civil war and violent anarchy). The reasons that lead people, and regimes, to tolerate those of whom they disapprove are complex and resist easy generalizations about individual motivations and complex political decisions.

Further complicating the relationship between these two terms is the fact that few commentators use them consistently. Many use "tolerance" to refer to an individual disposition or character trait, as opposed to toleration's political or legal focus, but such a definitional distinction—tolerance as individual and attitudinal, toleration as institutional and practice-oriented—is hardly universally accepted, and many authors use the terms interchangeably. An entire research tradition in political science locates "political tolerance" in survey respondents' self-reported willingness to support civil liberties for members of unpopular or marginalized groups, including social, political, religious, or sexual minorities. (Such legal and political concerns have long been described as forms of toleration.) That other languages lack English's two distinct terms can also complicate our understanding of works that originate outside of the English-speaking world.

For example, the first English edition of Voltaire's 1763 *Traité sur la Tolérance* appeared a year later under the title *A Treatise on Religious Toleration*.

To mitigate these terminological difficulties, whenever possible I use *toleration* to refer to political practices or institutional arrangements, and *tolerance* to refer to individual attitudes or beliefs. It is a terminological distinction that I have advocated for a number of years now (though, it must be said, without a great deal of success). However, many of the sources considered here—whether historical figures or contemporary critics—do not make such a distinction consistently, so keeping the terminology clear will be easier said than done.

Finally, the third challenge that bedevils writing about toleration: many assume that the history of toleration is necessarily connected with modern liberalism, liberal democracy, constitutional government, Christianity, or the "Western" political tradition. Those with a more sanguine view of the liberal tradition (a broad term for the dominant modern theory of government, which emphasizes individual rights, representative institutions, and market economies) associate toleration with all things praiseworthy in politics, including individual moral autonomy, limited government, and the core rights guaranteed by the liberal state, such as trial by jury and the liberties of conscience, press, speech, and assembly. The importance of early modern debates over religious toleration for liberal thinkers is difficult to overstate, since sixteenth- and seventeenth-century "wars of religion," and the presence of a variety of competing doctrines in society, set the political agenda that liberal theories have long sought to address. The overt or implicit triumphalism in many such accounts, however, misrepresents the historical record and obscures the persistence of exclusionary practices down to the present day in Western nations, to say nothing of pre-modern and non-Western exemplars of toleration.

By contrast, for other observers such a purported connection with the Western and liberal political traditions ties toleration to legacies of imperialism, colonialism, Eurocentrism, and related practices of domination and exclusion. As such, toleration has frequently been a target for critics of modern liberalism, condemned as unduly minimal and grudging when compared with more expansive terms like recognition or acceptance; and as overly complicit with the imperial systems that accompanied the emergence of modern liberal democracies. After all, tolerationist colonial regimes often loudly proclaimed the virtues of toleration and liberty while denying them to the native populations over which they ruled.

There is a degree of validity to both of these interpretations. Toleration has, indeed, long been considered a cardinal liberal commitment, endorsed by figures like John Locke (whose 1689 *Letter Concerning Toleration* is considered by many to be toleration's foundational text), John Stuart Mill, and John Rawls; and it has been applied to a range of social issues beyond religion in the years since its early modern emergence. But liberalism and toleration, while historically related in certain important ways, are hardly synonymous, and the connections between them are not necessary correlations. The liberal tradition emerged in early modern Europe in response to a number of important developments, including but by no means limited to religious violence between Catholics and Protestants and a corresponding rise in state power at the expense of ecclesiastical authority. But as many have noted, toleration as a way of dealing with the potentially destabilizing implications of diversity has appeared in places and at times far from the Western liberal tradition and well before the sixteenth century. Frequent trumpeting of the Christian and liberal origins of toleration tells only half (or, perhaps, less than half) of the story. Such Western triumphalism is both unremarkable—the modern concept of toleration is, in fact, rooted in European Christian debates—and deeply problematic, since toleration as a phenomenon is hardly limited to its modern and Christian origins.

Accounts that play up the Western and Christian dimensions of the history of toleration, which often remain focused on early modern Europe to the exclusion of other times, places, and actors, need to be supplemented with two other key aspects of the history of toleration and "the West": the existence of successful efforts to ensure peaceful coexistence in pre-modern and/or non-Western societies, and the extension of Western influence, often in far from tolerationist ways, through the exercise of colonial and imperial power. Critiques offered by toleration's detractors highlight the undeniable historical record of domination and violence practiced by European nations on those regions and peoples that they colonized (as well as their own people), with talk of toleration appearing either ironic or downright hypocritical. That said, it seems undeniable that toleration will continue to play a key role in the protracted struggles of marginalized groups for inclusion, offering a necessary, if not always sufficient, condition for liberty and civic membership across a wide range of settings.

Etymology and philosophy

Critics of toleration—and, indeed, even some of its defenders—have long pointed out that it carries with it a whiff of inherent judgment and negativity, the notion of enduring the presence of something one finds painful, noxious, distasteful, immoral, or even evil. As far back as 46 BCE, Cicero described the wise man as possessing the virtue of *tolerantia fortunae*, the capacity for enduring fortune or fate. The idea of toleration as bearing with something unpleasant is borne out by some of the basic definitions of the term; according to the *Oxford English Dictionary*, toleration represents the "action or practice of tolerating or allowing what is not actually approved," and to tolerate means to endure, sustain, allow, or permit. Such a view is illustrated graphically (and painfully) in Henry Cockeram's 1623 *English Dictionarie*, which described the Roman youth Gaius Mucius Scaevola as "sav[ing] his life by the patient toleration of the burning of his hand" during Rome's war with Clusium in the sixth century BCE.

Those who wish to probe the complex blend of disapproval and permission inherent in toleration remain indebted, nearly fifty years after its first publication, to Preston King's classic 1976 study, *Toleration*. King offered a conceptual analysis of toleration's component parts, identifying its essence in the simultaneous and apparently paradoxical presence of objection and permission, which demands an intentional exercise of self-restraint on the part of a would-be tolerator. More recently, in his monumental *Toleration in Conflict: Past and Present*, Rainer Forst built on King's pioneering formulation, presenting toleration as involving three main components. First, toleration contains an objection component, the existence of disapproval or negative judgments directed at beliefs or practices considered mistaken or harmful. Notwithstanding these objections, however, toleration also involves, secondly, an acceptance component, which provides countervailing reasons for tolerators to permit the groups that embrace those objectionable practices or beliefs. All versions of toleration have their limits—depending on the tolerator, depending on the thing(s) tolerated, depending on the context in which toleration is being discussed—and that outer limit makes up a third element, the rejection component: instances when the acceptance component no longer suffices to overcome objections and a practice or belief is deemed, quite literally, intolerable. This "rejection component" marks the limits of toleration.

Much more could be said about each of these three components of toleration. A great deal of ink has been spilled in attempts to clarify and justify the rejection component, things that ought not be tolerated. John Locke's denial of toleration to both Catholics (those "who... deliver themselves up to the protection and service of another Prince") and atheists represents one prominent example of this rejection component. More recently, the "paradox of tolerance," most often associated with Karl Popper, justifies the intolerance of intolerance as necessary for the preservation of tolerance. As Popper put it, "Unlimited tolerance must lead to the disappearance of tolerance."

It may be fairly clear how toleration differs from outright persecution—where we might say that the objection and rejection components go hand in hand—but how can it best be distinguished from other approaches to diversity, such as mere acquiescence or simple indifference? What sorts of reasons inspire people, or regimes, to permit the existence of practices and beliefs that they consider erroneous, or even evil? In addition to objection and rejection, the specific nature of the acceptance component has also come in for much analysis. Many who have written on the topic insist that, in order to qualify as proper toleration, such acceptance requires intentional, principled reasons. Put differently, they insist that true toleration requires robust, substantive, and reasonable justifications for extending guarantees to unpopular or marginalized groups. On such an account, toleration must be distinguished from simple battle fatigue, indifference, or resignation to the inevitability of diversity. It must involve a proactive decision on the part of government officials or regimes, a choice to protect rights.

Such attempts to differentiate toleration from other sorts of arrangements often take aim at the related, though distinct, notion of a *modus vivendi*: literally, a "way of living" together, the achievement of a basic level of coexistence characterized by a cessation of violence, whether based on a balance of power, a stalemate between warring parties, or simply a calculation that the costs of eradicating dissent are unacceptably high. These efforts aim to distinguish toleration from stalemate, or indifference, or passive acquiescence in the face of entrenched conflict, and are often driven by a desire to present it as a moral phenomenon and not merely a surrender to political realities. But while such attempts may be worthwhile philosophically speaking, it is undeniable that, historically speaking, many advances in the realm of toleration actually did begin as pragmatic, instrumental arrangements, which provided the necessary (though surely not the sufficient) conditions for further expansions of liberty.

The kind of minimal level of coexistence implied by the notion of a *modus vivendi* might not seem worthy of celebration from a twenty-first century perspective, but it surely represents an advance over violent conflict and persecution and reflects the attainment of a measure of social peace, even if a tenuous one, often at grave human cost. Such a tolerationist politics is built upon an appreciation that deeply held and fundamentally conflicting values are with us to stay. The historical development of religious toleration in the early modern world—to say nothing of the pre-modern and imperial regimes that sought to ensure the peaceful coexistence of the diverse groups under their control—is littered with *modus vivendi*-like arrangements, which facilitated minimal, pragmatic agreements to placate the various parties and bring peace out of religious strife. Often, though by no means always, such cessations of violence made the subsequent movement toward a more robustly pacific order possible.

What all of these varied aspects of the term point to is that toleration has long offered a degree of inclusion—often minimal, grudging, or partial—to those facing discrimination or outright persecution. Nonetheless, the power imbalances inherent in the term—the existence of a tolerator and a tolerated, with the tolerator offering permission or protection to the tolerated on the tolerator's terms—have led critics either to discount its significance or to highlight its undeniable imperfections. Toleration has frequently been characterized as a distinctly minimalist practice, grudgingly limited when compared with terms like freedom or liberty; a notion that merely involves putting up with people or practices that one opposes, rather than interrogating the nature of that disapproval, or attempting to move beyond it.

Indeed, the tolerationist language of restraint from repression often encourages such a less-than-ideal, glass half-empty evaluation. Even those sympathetic to toleration's importance and potential frequently admit that it offers neither a formula for social harmony nor a roadmap to utopia. We might say that toleration offers a degree of political or legal inclusion with one hand, while holding back fuller measures of acceptance or endorsement with the other (and furthermore, what looks like inclusion in one context may appear woefully inadequate in others). Toleration does not insist on expressions of good will, or endorsement of minoritized perspectives, and thus leaves itself open to charges that it lacks concern for fuller aspirations to equality and freedom.

As a result of this minimalist nature, toleration has generally been considered a "negative" liberty, most at home in political traditions such as classical liberalism and others that emphasize the importance of individual rights and limited government. Yet even minimal, negative liberties require positive governmental action for their enactment, and we should not underestimate the substantive demands that "negative" freedoms like toleration can place on rulers and regimes. Toleration may involve permitting unpopular forms of religious or other types of expression, and protecting individuals' rights to engage in such activities and to gather in peace with like-minded others. It thus provides a kind of benchmark or baseline from which further discussions of fuller liberty can begin. Such discussions will always reflect the power relationships, political possibilities, and background social conditions of their historical settings. Toleration is not an abstract thing, after all, but rather a constellation of particular groups in specific contexts, attempting to work out their relationships using the conceptual and political resources available to them to pursue their objectives.

Hence toleration is always relational in nature, embodied in concrete dynamics of power, and given widely varying institutional or political practices it may look rather different in different times and places. For some, toleration's appeal lies in its potential to serve a transitional role in suspending efforts at suppression while clearing the landscape, so to speak, to allow for the emergence of more robust notions of acceptance or equality. Such an approach no doubt appeals to the tolerated as promising improvements, if incremental, in their legal and political status. For others, such a transitional role offers an opportunity for the conversion of their erroneous neighbors away from their misguided or heretical beliefs, to bring them back into the fold, so to speak, using less bloody but hopefully more effective means. In each case, toleration represents a step on the road to something else.

Chapter 2
Before and beyond the Reformation

In his monumental *History of the Decline and Fall of the Roman Empire*, as he sought to account for the prosperity that characterized the reign of the Antonine emperors, Edward Gibbon pointed to Rome's religious policies, which allowed conquered provinces to "enjoy the religion of their ancestors." Gibbon offered the following portrait of that policy and the way that it shaped the capital city's religious and political landscape:

> The policy of the emperors and the senate, as far as it concerned religion, was happily seconded by the reflections of the enlightened, and by the habits of the superstitious, part of their subjects. The various modes of worship, which prevailed in the Roman world, were all considered by the people, as equally true; by the philosopher, as equally false; and by the magistrates, as equally useful. And thus toleration produced not only mutual indulgence, but even religious concord.... Rome, the capital of a great monarchy, was incessantly filled with subjects and strangers from every part of the world, who all introduced and enjoyed the favorite superstitions of their native country.

Whether or not these observations accurately portray historical realities—and historians have long taken issue with many of Gibbon's claims—they provide insight into several important considerations about toleration. As a tool of statecraft, Gibbon suggested that toleration was particularly amenable to imperial systems that contained diverse populations, an especially useful strategy for magistrates concerned to pacify potentially restive provinces. (Toleration as a tool of empire—from Rome and early Persia to British India and beyond—is a recurrent theme in many different historical contexts.) About religion itself—the thing being tolerated—Gibbon emphasized its appeal to different groups on different levels, using the term "superstition" twice to suggest that religion appealed in one way to the masses while being discreetly disdained by elites. Also important for understanding toleration is Gibbon's description of Rome ("the capital of a great monarchy") as a cosmopolitan city, and thus a place where practical considerations of public life militated against persecution and facilitated a culture of coexistence. Insofar as Roman toleration allowed "subjects and strangers from every part of the world" to enjoy their "favorite superstitions," it represented a key ingredient of civil peace.

Although the lion's share of academic commentary on toleration locates its origins (as both a concept and a practice) in the sixteenth- and seventeenth-century Reformation, Counter-Reformation, and European wars of religion, strategies for pursuing peaceful coexistence between groups with histories of conflict and animosity neither began with Protestant-Catholic relations in early modern Europe nor appeared solely in "Western" contexts. Many pre-modern and non-Western antecedents and alternatives exist, and they allow for a richer and more nuanced story of toleration to be told, one in which political thinkers and practical politicians worked to secure civil peace between diverse groups.

Cyrus II of Persia

In her 2003 Nobel Lecture upon receiving the Nobel Peace Prize, human rights activist Shirin Ebadi described herself thus: "I am an Iranian. A descendent of Cyrus the Great. The very emperor who proclaimed at the pinnacle of power 2,500 years ago that 'he would not reign over the people if they did not wish it.' And he promised not to force any person to change his religion and faith and guaranteed freedom for all." In tying her own decorated work as a campaigner for democracy and the rights of women, children, and refugees to Cyrus's legacy, Ebadi made a powerful statement not only about her own commitments but also about Cyrus's place in historical memory as an exemplar of religious freedom. (That she was apparently quoting from an internet source that inaccurately translated the famed "Cyrus Cylinder," a Babylonian artifact of baked clay excavated in nineteenth-century Iraq that represents an important source of information about Cyrus's career, does not undermine Ebadi's larger point about the widespread admiration of Cyrus and his legacy.)

2. The Cyrus Cylinder, a clay cylinder containing an account of Cyrus's genealogy and conquest of Babylon in 539 BCE, was excavated in Mesopotamia in 1879. It presents Cyrus's rule as benevolent, favored by the gods, and respectful of the various religious communities over which he ruled.

Cyrus II (also known as "the Great"), founder of the Achaemenid Empire and the ruler under whom the Persians conquered Babylon in 539 BCE, reigned over a vast empire encompassing much of Southwest Asia and North Africa. Although we know little about Cyrus's life and career, Babylonian and Jewish texts alike present him as a magnanimous and heroic ruler, treating his conquered peoples far less harshly than had his oppressive and degenerate predecessor Nabonidus, who had neglected the traditional religious observances. Cyrus, by contrast, established peace in the land and returned to the regular observance of those rituals. "The city of Babylon and all its cult-centres I maintained in well-being," Cyrus announces in the cylinder's account. "May all the gods, whom I have brought into their cities... say words in my favor."

Cyrus left no records that would allow us to know about his personal religious beliefs: he may have worshipped Mithra, the sun god, or Ahura Mazda, the chief Zoroastrian deity. According to the account on the cylinder, his virtue attracted the attention of Marduk, the patron deity of Babylon. Marduk disapproved of those ruling Babylon, and "looked through all the countries, searching for a righteous ruler [and] pronounced the name of Cyrus... declar[ing] him to become the ruler of all the world." The cylinder provides a fragmentary Babylonian account of the Persian conquest, presenting Cyrus (in his own words) as one who "returned the gods... to their places.... The whole of their peoples I assembled, and I returned them to their homes." Cyrus also figures prominently in the Jewish tradition, where he is celebrated as the ruler who invited the Jews to return from their Babylonian exile and made possible the reconstruction of the Temple in Jerusalem. In Isaiah 44:28, for example, the Lord says of Cyrus, "He is my shepherd and will accomplish all that I please; he will say of Jerusalem, 'Let it be rebuilt,' and of the temple, 'Let its foundations be laid.'"

Such actions would have been broadly consistent with what is known generally of Cyrus's religious policies. Given the polytheistic milieu in which he operated as well as the more general imperatives of smooth rulership over diverse populations, which called not only for empire building but also attending to alliances and providing for the efficient administration of conquered lands, Cyrus apparently allowed the conquered peoples under his rule to continue to worship their own gods. Those policies mirror his more general approach to ruling, which seems to have involved minimal changes to local administration and economic life. There is no evidence that Cyrus promoted religious diversity as an intrinsic good, but he certainly saw the political wisdom of an imperial policy that permitted conquered peoples to continue their own religious practices. In this regard, his toleration seems to represent primarily a means toward the end of imperial control and social peace. In fact, however, he took things one step further, inserting himself into the religious traditions of a number of those conquered peoples as a way of buttressing his legitimacy as a ruler. The Cyrus Cylinder portrays the Babylonian god Marduk favoring Cyrus and choosing him to rule over the earth; Jewish sources laud Cyrus as the Lord's "anointed one... whom he has taken by the hand" (Isaiah 45:1–2) and guaranteed victory.

Ashoka

Turning to South Asia, and shifting the temporal focus ahead several centuries, leads us to Ashoka (sometimes rendered Asoka), who ruled the Mauryan Empire on the Indian subcontinent from roughly 268 to 232 BCE. According to legend, Ashoka renounced violence as a kind of penance after his bloody conquest of the Kalinga region on India's eastern coastal plain. Following that renunciation, Ashoka turned his attention to securing the peaceful coexistence of the many sects that inhabited his kingdom, a policy he called *Dhamma*, or right behavior, in accordance with his Buddhist commitments. (Whether Ashoka professed Buddhism before the Kalinga war or came to Buddhism as part of the ethical reckoning that followed it remains unclear.) He announced those intentions in a series of inscriptions engraved onto large rocks in places designed to command the attention of passersby. These "rock edicts" form a significant part of Ashoka's importance to the history of toleration.

Ashoka's rock edicts cover a wide range of issues, including imperial administration, animal sacrifice, ceremonial observances, and the renunciation of violent imperial expansion. For the purposes at hand, the seventh and twelfth edicts are the most relevant. The seventh edict enjoined members of diverse sects to live peacefully with each other, expressing Ashoka's wish that "everywhere in his dominions members of all religions and sects may reside together and harmoniously." Such harmony was grounded in a universalistic understanding of human aspirations to right living ("all desire in common to achieve mastery of the senses and purity of mind"), while acknowledging the variety of desires and passions that drive individuals.

The twelfth edict began by announcing that Ashoka "reverences persons of all sects" and values above all else "an increase in the spiritual strength of the followers of all religions." The edict addressed the tendency for divisive speech to foster religious division and commanded "the guarding of one's speech so as to avoid the extolling of one's own religion to the decrying of the religion of another," as a primary means of pursuing increased spiritual strength and the "concord of all religions." The edict thus recommended a kind of self-restraint on the part of individual adherents, which benefited the reputation not only of individuals but also the religious communities to which they belonged. Ashoka's desired outcome—a "concord of all religions"—linked the policy to the pursuit of civil peace among a diverse population.

Ashoka's aspirations regarding the religious diversity that characterized his empire, as made clear in the rock edicts, have been described using such terms as "religious tolerance," "toleration," "freedom of religious expression," and "principled" or "peaceful" coexistence. Even more expansively, some have viewed the rock edicts as pointing beyond toleration and approaching something like goodwill or mutual respect. Regardless of the specific terms used, Ashoka's edicts promoted an ideal in which a variety of religious communities enjoy harmonious coexistence, not merely through permission granted by state authorities and institutions (what we might call a "vertical" power relationship), but also through efforts at securing "horizontal" concord between groups. Many of the specifics of Ashoka's system of *Dhamma* remain unclear, and it seems to have focused more on norms of civility than on explicit doctrine or rituals. The rock edicts illustrate Ashoka's attempts to model such norms and to display compassionate concern for the various religious groups within his realm.

Akbar

The third Mughal emperor, Akbar, who ruled India for four decades beginning in 1556, has captured the imagination of public officials, scholars, poets, and novelists alike. Akbar was celebrated by British East India Company officials during the eighteenth century as an enlightened, tolerationist autocrat, and by Alfred Lord Tennyson, whose *Akbar's Dream* includes a set of notes in which the poet writes that Akbar's "tolerance of religions and his abhorrence of religious persecution put our Tudors to shame." Akbar also plays a central role in Salman Rushdie's 2008 novel, *The Enchantress of Florence*. Nobel Prize-winning economist and philosopher Amartya Sen has heaped praise on Akbar as well, describing his reign as offering a powerful Indian defense of toleration and state neutrality toward religion.

Akbar's religious biography is a complex one: a spiritual awakening at the age of twenty led him to abolish religious taxes on non-Muslims; a passion for religious discussion and disputation motivated him to construct a House of Worship (Ibādat Khāna) and a Hall of Private Audience (Diwan-i-Khas) in his capital city of Fatehpur Sikri to house such conversations, which Akbar personally oversaw; increasingly mystical experiences due to the influence of Sufism; an open breach with the realm's Islamic authorities in his forties; and the attempt to create a new, syncretic religion, Dīn-i Ilāhī (Faith of the Divine), which drew from the empire's many faiths, during the final decades of his life. This last development led to a series of proclamations in the early 1590s, including that "No man should be interfered with on account of his religion, and anyone was to be allowed to go over to any religion he pleased," and "If any of the infidels chose to build a church, or synagogue, or idol-temple... no one was to hinder him."

Although Dīn-i Ilāhī appears to have attracted few converts, the example of Akbar's House of Worship and Hall of Private Audience has led to his valorization as a proponent of toleration and interreligious dialogue. Perhaps not surprisingly, Akbar's religious syncretism and enthusiasm for interreligious dialogue apparently led to tension with more orthodox Muslims, leading many to consider Akbar an apostate. Some observers have celebrated Akbar's example as evoking the tolerationist sentiments of his predecessor Ashoka. Other commentators on Indian affairs have invoked Akbar's example in arguing against portrayals of the past that see the nation as essentially Hindu, or as characterized by more or less unceasing war between religious communities. Still others have offered more tempered views of a ruler characterized by ruthless ambition, and pointed out that even his proclamations about religious freedom contained limitations and exceptions, including prohibitions on Hindu women converting to Islam.

Medieval Europe

The tolerationist careers of Cyrus, Ashoka, and Akbar emerge out of non-European contexts. But medieval Europe—long dismissed as a monolithic "persecuting society" characterized by the Inquisition, persecution of Jews, and policies of exclusion and oppression directed at other religiously heterodox groups—also

3. In an illustration from the *Akbarnama* (The History of Akbar) by Abu'l-Fazl, Akbar, the third Mughal emperor, presides over an interreligious dialogue at the Ibādat Khāna, a meetinghouse in Akbar's capital city of Fatehpur Sikri.

produced a number of exemplary cases in the history of toleration. After all, regardless of official rhetoric, imposing religious uniformity was simply impossible for most authorities, even had they wanted to do so (and many, in fact, were less than zealous to do so). As a result, a fair amount of de facto toleration prevailed in many places, with Jews and Muslims often permitted to maintain their distinctive traditions even while authorities attempted to suppress Christian "heretics." Even without explicit philosophical doctrines endorsing diversity for its own sake, rulers often sought to permit, and even encourage, the presence of minority populations within their borders, be it for the pragmatic concerns about smooth administration we saw above with Cyrus, or nascent ideas about respecting difference and the realities of interdependence, as seems to have been the case with Ashoka and Akbar.

Even church authorities, often portrayed as ruthlessly dedicated to stamping out heterodoxy above all else, frequently displayed little reluctance about allowing debate over contested points of Christian doctrine or practice, though they generally sought to keep such debates out of the public eye. Accordingly, themes of toleration and concordance appear in the thought of a wide range of medieval Christian figures, including Christine de Pizan, John Wycliffe, John of Salisbury, the French envoy William of Rubruck (sent by Louis IX as a thirteenth-century ambassador to Mongol courts), Marsiglio of Padua, and Nicholas of Cusa. Although the rarefied air occupied by many of these church figures—who often privately circulated manuscripts voicing their dissenting perspectives and participated in dialogues populated largely by elite churchmen—might undermine their relevance for broader audiences, the search for agreement across differences and commitment to dialogue and debate as key to the search for truth give them direct relevance to the broader history of toleration.

In addition to the visions of toleration and forbearance offered by these medieval thinkers, we can look to specific practical contexts where diverse religious communities lived side by side, often within larger empires, and developed practices and strategies of coexistence.

Medieval Spain and the *convivencia*

Observers seeking insights into the potential for peaceful religious coexistence have long looked to the lived experience of Muslims, Christians, and Jews in medieval Spain as a concrete example of interreligious harmony, or at least an absence of overt hostility and violence. In his 1948 *España en su historia*, the Spanish historian Américo Castro described the system under the Almohad Caliphate, the Nasrid dynasty, and other Muslim rulers between the twelfth and fifteenth centuries as "la convivencia religiosa" (religious coexistence). Castro credited a culture of harmony between the three faiths, in which a "basic position of tolerance" ensured social peace and facilitated economic prosperity, with contributing to the broader development of Spanish history and culture. (Castro was not the first to make these points; during the Spanish Civil War, the Franco regime had also evoked the past glory of al-Andalus and used the *convivencia* to justify Spanish colonialism.)

The term "convivencia" quickly sparked debate about the precise nature of inter-religious contact and imperial policy across the Iberian peninsula, as well as the degree to which the facts of coexistence, such as we know them, justify the term's pacific implications. Those who celebrated the *convivencia* described it as a glorious era of tolerance and cultural harmony, facilitated by a governing structure (known as the *dhimma* system) that made allowances for *dhimmi*, or "protected peoples," to live securely provided they acknowledged their Islamic rulers' authority and paid an additional tax. (Practices like these stretched back to the early days of the Muslim community in Medina.) More skeptical accounts stressed economic interconnection and pragmatic considerations as the real engine of social tranquility, and acknowledged that these economic relationships took place against the constant backdrop of (actual or threatened) communal violence. But of course not everyone saw the *convivencia* as an example to be aspired to; even more critical responses viewed the notion of the *convivencia* as an oversimplified, idealized, and romanticized picture of an imperial reality in which Christians and Jews lived on the terms dictated from above, in a top-down manner, by their Muslim rulers.

It is undeniable that these three religious communities inhabited a diverse society where, in many places, their members lived, worshipped, and did business side-by-side with members of other communities. It is also undeniable that such interactions always involved some degree of mutual collaboration along with a healthy dose of competition and communal mistrust. Although the system did break down at times, the rule, rather than the exception, that prevailed in the Iberian context was one in which Muslim rulers tolerated non-Muslims within their borders.

Regardless of the precise nature of the Iberian *convivencia*, however, the fall of Granada to the forces of Ferdinand and Isabella, and the final victory of the Christian *Reconquista* in 1492—which soon yielded decrees that banished the realm's Jews and ordered Muslims to convert to Christianity or face expulsion, if not death—signaled a bitter end to any sort of pacific religious coexistence. The transformation of mosques into Christian churches across Spain—some through demolition, others through dramatic construction that overlaid Christian onto previously Muslim worship spaces, as in the mosque-cathedral of Córdoba—provided a visible manifestation of the replacement of Muslim by Christian authority. Nonetheless, the example of the *convivencia* retains a powerful symbolic importance regarding the potential for peaceful coexistence between rival communities in a pluralistic society under a common ruler. It has also assumed particular importance for those seeking to envision a multiethnic Spanish future, as activists

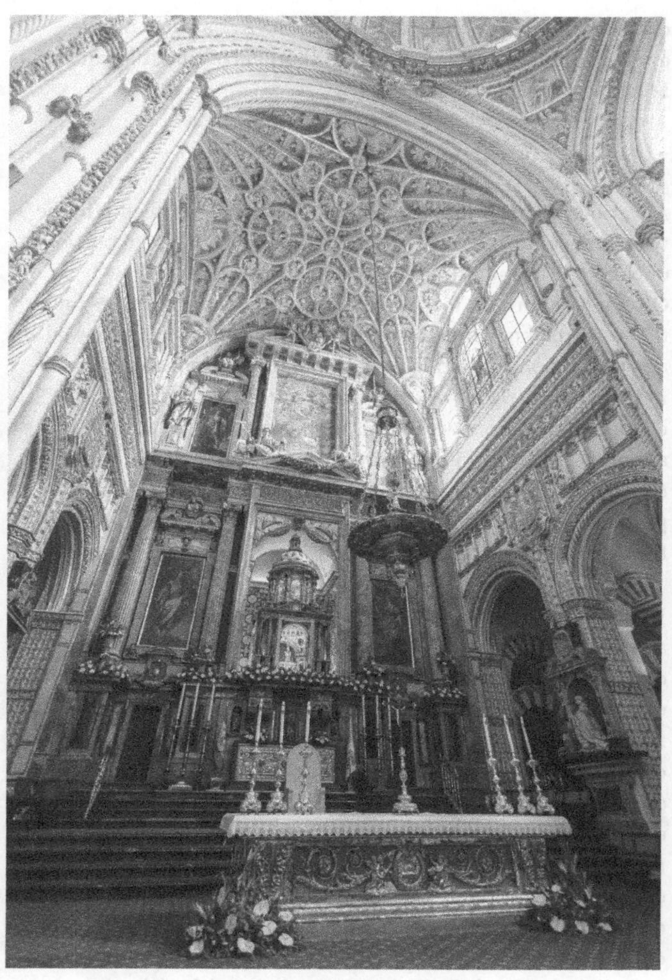

4. An interior view of the mosque-cathedral of Córdoba displays the intertwined nature of the Christian and Islamic legacies in medieval Iberia.

continue to draw on the symbolism of the Andalusian past to evoke a tradition of toleration at the borders of Christian and Muslim worlds.

The Ottoman millet system

At various points over its long history from the fourteenth to the twentieth centuries, the Ottoman Empire encompassed portions of North Africa, southern Europe, and western Asia. The Ottomans' approach to managing the diverse communities under their control, known as the millet system, has long been viewed as a potential non-Western alternative to the predominantly individualistic, rights-oriented justifications for toleration commonly advanced within the liberal tradition. Much of this attention has been animated by the increasingly visible politics of cultural and linguistic diversity within modern nation-states, particularly after the breakup of the Soviet Union and the end of the Cold War.

Under the millet system, in ways broadly similar to the Iberian arrangement sketched out just above, Ottoman rulers allowed officially recognized religious communities a significant measure of autonomy over their own affairs, including worship and religious rituals as well as the opportunity to retain their distinctive legal systems, in return for payment of a dedicated tax and a recognition of Ottoman political sovereignty. At its most effective, the system provided an effective power-sharing mechanism and facilitated smooth relationships between the empire's Muslim rulers and their non-Muslim subjects. The clear demarcation of communal boundaries allowed for the allocation of responsibilities within each millet, of which there were several, including the Greek Orthodox, Armenian, and Jewish communities. Although the millet system drew support from within the Islamic tradition, with its *dhimma* contract aimed at ensuring the protection of non-Muslims under Muslim rulers, it also contained a strong pragmatic streak. Allowing communities to organize their internal affairs in accord with their own customs and traditions made smooth administration of the empire that much easier.

Some version of a millet-like system was also adopted by other imperial powers, most notably, though to a lesser extent, the Habsburg Empire, where Catholicism played a dominant role and thus framed the limits of the system. Vestiges of the millet system continue to the present day, to a greater or lesser degree, in places like Egypt, Lebanon, Israel, and Turkey, and in the relationship between the Iraqi state and its Kurdish population. Additional contemporary arrangements with some affinities to millet systems may be found in the United States government's relationships with Native American tribes, the status of American religious minorities like the Amish and Mennonites, and Muslims living in the United Kingdom. As these experiences show, though millet-like arrangements can indicate a clear aspiration toward religious coexistence, such systems are fraught with challenges, and the protection of religious or cultural minorities is by no means guaranteed.

Despite enthusiasm among contemporary commentators about the potential for millet-like arrangements to address twenty-first-century challenges, critics have pointed to a number of factors that raise questions about their contemporary viability. Individual members of the Ottoman millets, after all, had no rights against their own religious communities and little recourse against the exercise of power by those who headed those communities. Throwing further doubt on the contemporary utility of the millet example is the obvious fact that the broader political context in which the millet system operated was, to say the least, not based on notions of democratic equality or individual rights.

The Spanish and Ottoman models—*convivencia* and millet—clearly attract attention from political thinkers and public figures looking for new approaches from outside dominant, European traditions as they attempt to deal with a resurgence in ethnic conflicts in the post-Cold War context. As Gibbon saw in Rome, so others have seen in Iberia or the Ottoman lands: given fortuitous circumstances, the empire, as a political form, can clearly facilitate schemes of toleration.

Early Christianity

Long before it became the official religion of the Roman Empire and achieved hegemonic political influence, the Christian community was an excluded and at times persecuted group, scattered around the Mediterranean and North Africa. We might expect representatives of such a marginalized group to call for toleration, and indeed they did. The importance of such Church Fathers as Tertullian, Cyprian, and Lactantius lies less in the success of their pleas for religious liberty (they were not always successful, to put it mildly) than as expressions of widely held views among leaders of the early church, and for their influence on later Christian tolerationists as well. During the Reformation and early modern period, quoting Tertullian and Lactantius became not only a way to establish one's Christian and tolerationist bona fides, but also a key element of a widespread argument that true religion lay in inner conviction, impervious to coercion, non-seditious and non-treasonous.

Early Christian toleration arguments were simultaneously defenses of themselves from claims that they were politically dangerous or disloyal and attempts to articulate an ethos of forbearance as a distinguishing feature within the Christian community. Tertullian, an early Church Father from Carthage, asserted the right of his community to gather for worship as "a fundamental human right, a privilege of nature, that every man should worship according to his own convictions: one man's religion neither harms nor helps another man. It is assuredly no part of religion to compel religion." Addressing himself to those within the church rather than to political authorities, Cyprian, who served as Bishop of Carthage for roughly a decade during the mid-third century CE, called Christians to humility and gentleness in their dealings with each other, citing Paul's exhortations to charity in 1 Corinthians 13 and Ephesians 4:2–3. (Such appeals would become even more significant and powerful in the early modern period, when both rulers and subjects claimed membership in the Christian community.) The Church Father Lactantius, to whom the emperor Constantine entrusted the education of his son and who advised Constantine on imperial religious policy, denounced the persecution of Christians, insisting in his *Divine Institutes* that "if you wish to defend religion by bloodshed, and by tortures, and by guilt, it will no longer be defended, but will be polluted and profaned."

Much changed, to be sure, beginning with the emperor Galerius's Edict of Serdica in 311 CE, which ended the persecution of Christians initiated by his predecessor Diocletian, and Constantine's conversion to Christianity a year later. Constantine, in turn, issued the Edict of Milan in 313 CE, which granted "to the Christians and others" permission "to observe that religion which each preferred." The justification Constantine offered might strike modern ears as a bit self-serving, not to mention less than religiously confident—"whence any Divinity whatsoever in the seat of the heavens may be propitious and kindly disposed to us and all who are placed under our rule"—but it represented a monumental shift in imperial religious politics. With the Edict of Thessalonica, issued by Theodosius I in 380 CE, which established Nicene Christianity as the religion of the empire, the once-persecuted sect had officially arrived. Then again, for many later Christian tolerationists, the transformation of Christianity from a marginalized community to the official religion of a sprawling empire represented a calamitous outcome that imperiled the core elements of the Christian faith, facilitated the persecution of heretics, and corrupted the church with political power. In the words of Roger Williams, "Christianity fell asleep in Constantine's bosom."

The individual rulers, religious leaders, and institutional arrangements laid out above do not exhaust the historical record of times and places where communities marked by conflict have sought, and at times attained, peaceful coexistence and a cessation of violence. Many more examples could be cited as well, including the Shi'a Fatimid Caliphate in North Africa (tenth to twelfth centuries BCE) and the Central Asian conqueror Tamerlane (or Timur), whose legendary reputation was hailed in Restoration England. In his *General History of the Turks*, Richard Knolles described Tamerlane as "disliking of no man for his religion whatsoever, so as he did worship but one only God, creator of heaven and Earth, and of all that therein is." Before the Reformation and beyond the borders of Europe, aspirations for peaceful coexistence drove numerous efforts to facilitate social harmony in conditions of religious and ethnic diversity.

Chapter 3
Early modern foundations

The European debate over toleration grew increasingly politically contested and philosophically sophisticated during the early modern period. Although John Locke's 1689 *Letter Concerning Toleration* has received an inordinate amount of the attention on this topic, due not only to Locke's importance to English politics and philosophy but also to his influence on the American founders, Locke is merely the tip—and, to be frank, not the most interesting tip—of a much larger tolerationist iceberg. A more complete account, even one confined to Locke's English context, would include other well-known thinkers such as John Milton and rulers such as Oliver Cromwell and King James II, each of whom (regardless of what one might think of their larger legacies) sought to expand the frontiers of religious liberty. It would also include practical political actors and controversialists whose careers spanned the Atlantic, such as Roger Williams, the English Separatist and founder of Rhode Island, and William Penn, the Quaker theorist and activist who founded Pennsylvania after a decade of unsuccessful efforts at securing toleration in England.

Casting a wider net across Europe, a thorough account of toleration's emergence in the early modern era would also consider Italian, French, Dutch, and German thinkers. Even more importantly, perhaps, it would incorporate the efforts of countless members of marginalized sects—names far less well-known centuries later—who relentlessly agitated, from their own understandings of the importance of religious commitment, for individuals to be free to fulfil their moral and religious obligations as their consciences dictated. Finally, it would encompass the (again, countless) local leaders who negotiated tolerationist schemes of coexistence between diverse religious groups in localities far from royal courts and ecclesiastical synods. There was never just one toleration debate, but rather there were many, in specific places and at specific times; participants in those debates deployed whichever arguments (scriptural, epistemological, historical, or pragmatic) they thought would achieve their desired ends.

Not only did religious and political dissent provide the impetus for conflict, civil war, and regime change across Europe during the sixteenth and seventeenth centuries, it also fired migration to the Americas—an eighteenth-century English pamphlet referred to New England and Pennsylvania as "peopled by our persecution"—as well as the Caribbean. These developments were crucial contributors to the emergence of toleration in matters of religion, which formed the basis for the later emergence of still broader notions of liberty (and also for European colonialism). Such factors serve as a useful reminder that toleration was never a self-evident good and that its attainment was by no means a foregone conclusion. Proponents of toleration had to contend with powerful political, religious, ideological, and social actors who offered cogent arguments against their proposals. Tolerationists asked their opponents, in a sense, to trust them that the severing of a centuries-old association between church and state would result not in chaos and anarchy but in a more peaceful social order and a purer form of religious experience. The widespread achievement of a measure of toleration in early modern Europe, and its elevation to a central plank in the liberal democratic tradition, only came after protracted struggles on several continents.

Reformation roots and unintended consequences

The route from the sixteenth-century Protestant Reformation to the emergence of early modern religious toleration was a complex and circuitous one, evidence of the power of unintended consequences and the explosively intertwined nature of political and religious conflict. Martin Luther's ferocious critique of Catholic doctrine and practice, which began as a call for reform but quickly grew into a much more thoroughgoing and bitter set of disputes, garnered support from both religiously minded sympathizers and civil rulers, many of whom endorsed the movement in pursuit of their own political interests. As a result, the Reformation played an important, if not always intended, role in fostering the growth of religious pluralism, and demonstrated the ways in which such pluralism, given fortuitous circumstances, can lead to religious toleration, which—again, given fortuitous circumstances—can lead to broader notions of liberty across a range of domains.

The multifaceted upheavals that spread across Europe during the sixteenth century, initiated by Luther's critique but spreading well beyond it, were widespread and profound. Across a range of settings—Luther and the German princes who supported him, Henry VIII in England, the Inquisition in Spain and elsewhere, Huguenot (French Protestant)-Catholic conflict in France, the growing opposition to Spanish rule in the Netherlands—the Reformation transformed the ecclesiastical and political map of early modern Europe. It upended established regimes, fostering incipient nationalism and the consolidation of state power, often at the expense of ecclesiastical authority. In doing so, it effectively undermined many of the traditional justifications for persecution; it also opened space for new religious communities to take root.

Henry's break with Rome lacked the important theological dimensions central to Luther's attack on the papacy: the English king was, to put it mildly, no fan of Luther and had been named Defender of the Faith by Pope Leo X in 1521 for his attacks on Lutheranism. But Henry wanted a male heir and thus needed the divorce that he believed could make that possible. Subsequent events in the English Reformation—the halting Protestantization of the English church during the short reign of Edward VI; its near erasure by the Catholic Mary I, whose efforts at returning the realm to the papal fold might well have succeeded had she not died just four years into her reign; and the eventual Elizabethan settlement, which created the (Protestant) Church of England—shaped not only the contours of English politics but also those of the British Empire well into the modern era.

Across the Channel, France endured violent conflict between Huguenots and Catholics for much of the second half of the sixteenth century. The collapse of a short-lived Edict of Toleration issued in 1562, which had provided Huguenots with a modicum of legal recognition, initiated the French Wars of Religion, with atrocities including the St. Bartholomew's Day Massacre, a 1572 slaughter of Paris's Protestants perpetrated by the capital's Catholics. In 1598 Henri IV issued the Edict of Nantes, which sought peaceful coexistence through a series of military, judicial, and geographic accommodations between the realm's religious communities. (The edict also expressed a hope that a reprieve from persecution would unify the kingdom religiously once again.) The 1568 outbreak of a revolt against Spanish rule in the Netherlands offered yet another example of the explosive intertwining of religion, politics, and rule in the wake of the Reformation.

Few Reformation figures endorsed toleration as a general principle. Most were primarily concerned with ensuring that their own group's religious truth claims be permitted, so that they might either eradicate the error they saw all around them or convert their rivals to the "true" faith. Yet the eruption of religious discord made a measure of compromise and coexistence necessary, if for no other reason than as a recognition of political realities and the persistence of religious diversity on the ground. Pragmatic, practical considerations about the perceived necessity of tolerating the "error" of others would often, over the long term, grow to a more robust endorsement of the advantages of peaceful coexistence between rival faith communities.

Luther, Erasmus, Christian humanism, and toleration

The figures of Martin Luther and Desiderius Erasmus cast a long shadow over the early modern politics of religion. Neither man endorsed toleration per se, but each played an integral role in shaping the religiously pluralistic world that would emerge in the Reformation's aftermath and in which debates over toleration would come to dominate political life.

Luther's attacks on church doctrine and policy unleashed a storm of social and political unrest, raising questions of political obedience and the limits of political authority over church affairs to a fever pitch. His treatise *On Secular Authority* (1523) drew a sharp distinction between the kingdom of God and the kingdom of the world, insisting that the latter's purpose was "to bring about external peace and prevent evil deeds." Luther denied the legitimacy of attempts to compel belief, since "every man is responsible for his own faith" and "no one has power over the soul but God." That said, Luther emphasized biblical teachings about political obedience (Romans 13, 1 Peter 2: 13–17), and his strong defense of political authority and abhorrence of social instability led him to denounce the 1524 uprising of German peasants. A subsequent work, *Against the Murderous, Thieving Hordes of Peasants* (1525)—the title, though perhaps not of Luther's choosing, accurately communicates its message—led to accusations of betrayal by the uprising's leaders, some of whose ecclesiastical, economic, social, and political grievances coincided with Luther's own critiques.

If Luther's efforts laid the foundation for political upheaval and an ultimate rupture of the church, Erasmus too played a central role in theological and ecclesiastical debate, and he would also leave a powerful and enduring legacy. Erasmus was deeply influenced by—and, in turn, himself influenced—the Renaissance humanist tradition, which spread from Italy to northern Europe during the late fifteenth and early sixteenth centuries. His approach to religious reform grew out of this humanism, including his advocacy for returning to original biblical texts (Erasmus published his edition of the Greek and Latin New Testament in 1516), his commitment to speech and debate as integral to the search for truth, and his reluctance to engage in rancorous disputes over theologically speculative topics. These qualities led Erasmus to stress the importance of a small number of "fundamentals of faith," distinct from *adiaphora*, or "indifferent things" about which reasonable Christians could disagree, as a way to reconcile believers with differing understandings of Christian belief and practice.

Erasmus pleaded for moderation in the conduct of disputes, drawing on the humanist tradition's view of force as bestial and an unworthy way of engaging with creatures created in the image of God (an image he took from Cicero, among others). His more general aspiration to *concordia* and harmony led him to a decidedly un-Lutheran emphasis on civil dialogue and to attempt to lower the rhetorical temperature in disputes over the nature of true Christianity and church policy. Although he criticized corruption in the church and sympathized with aspects of Luther's proposed reforms, Erasmus sought (ultimately, without success) to avoid a wholesale rupture.

The humanist legacy that Erasmus cultivated was carried forward by such thinkers as the Italian polymath Jacob Acontius and the French theologian Sebastian Castellio. These two thinkers shared Erasmus's commitment to dialogue and his belief that words and persuasive speech, not coercion, should settle religious controversies; celebrated virtues like charity, moderation, and forbearance; and continued efforts to distinguish essentials of faith from *adiaphora*. Central to this undertaking were efforts to reduce the number of such fundamentals, thus expanding the topics on which reasonable disagreement might proceed (and thus, perhaps, on which toleration might be secured). In Castellio's words, "It is sufficient to accept the fundamental points of true religion...provided a man...repent of his former evil life and resolve firmly not to return to it again." Or, as Acontius put it in his *Satans Stratagems*: "Men may be saved, though they misunderstand some points, and hold some errors."

This insistence that dialogue and debate are essential elements of the search for truth, and that such a search requires an acknowledgment of human fallibility, would remain central to much subsequent writing on toleration, from John Milton's *Areopagitica* (1644) through John Stuart Mill's *On Liberty* (1859). As Castellio put it in *Concerning Heretics*, in an argument that later appeared in *On Liberty*, "he who persecutes may quite as well be mistaken as the one who is persecuted."

Toleration debates in early modern Europe

The Reformation's upheavals prefigured the emergence of sophisticated debates over the limits of legitimate political and ecclesiastical authority, the nature of religious belief, and the boundaries of acceptable toleration. From a twenty-first century perspective, these controversies may not look particularly expansive: they focused primarily on gaining worship rights and ending legal penalties for gathering with fellow believers; and they proceeded largely within Christian—and, in many places, Protestant—parameters. That said, we should not overstate the degree to which Catholics and Protestants considered each other as fellow members of a common "religion"; Protestants routinely referred to the pope as "Antichrist," and in the Edict of Nantes Henri IV referred repeatedly to the "so-called Reformed religion."

Nor should we overlook the important arguments over the toleration of Jews in majority-Christian societies, which formed the larger context for George Washington's noted 1790 letter to the Hebrew Congregation in Newport. Long on the receiving end of antisemitic vitriol as well as economic and social discrimination, Jews presented an especially vivid example of the power imbalances inherent in the idea of toleration, which presumes a clearly distinguishable tolerator and tolerated. Despite these undeniable facts and the ongoing salience of Christian antisemitism as a primary obstacle to Jews' political enfranchisement, the presence of Christian philosemitism, such as we see in a figure like Oliver Cromwell (who supported the readmission of Jews to England on millenarian grounds, in which the Jews' conversion to Christianity would hasten Jesus's Second Coming) shows the complexity of Jewish-Christian history in Europe, and serves as a counterpoint to the relentless Christian focus that dominated much of the history of toleration.

Regardless of how restricted they might appear to later generations, however, these toleration debates proved to be foundational to the development of modern politics in Europe, North America, and—through the global spread of European ideas via colonial and imperial systems—around the world. They would also provide a conceptual framework for later thinkers to expand toleration into domains beyond religion. If toleration has a global dimension in the twenty-first century, it owes that character, in large part, to these early modern debates.

The forms and venues in which tolerationists pressed their case in the early modern world were as varied as the geographical locations in which the debates took place. Tolerationist arguments appeared in learned theological and philosophical tomes, in clandestine pamphlets printed on underground presses, in broadsheets and newspapers passed from hand to hand, and in sermons and orations delivered before congregations, monarchs, and legislatures. They were deployed among elite audiences in formal disputations, in bitterly contested public debates and acrimonious courtrooms, and in the lived experiences of members of countless communities across Europe. They grew out of revulsion over events like the 1572 St. Bartholomew's Day Massacre and the 1553 execution of Michael Servetus for heresy (an execution overseen by John Calvin), which occasioned Castellio's *Concerning Heretics* a year later and Acontius's *Satans Stratagems* in 1565. And a broader look at post-Reformation Europe makes clear that toleration represented not only campaigns on behalf of individuals and dissenting religious communities—struggles embraced by many modern tolerationist regimes—but also informed growing rivalries between emerging nation-states and ecclesiastical authorities.

Scriptural and theological arguments

Early modern toleration debates took place in professedly Christian societies (albeit deeply divided ones), proceeded from broadly Christian assumptions, and involved the deployment of vast scriptural arsenals. Tolerationists relied first and foremost on Jesus's example and ministry: he said virtually nothing about government, proclaiming that his kingdom was "not of this world" (John 18:36); he refused to call down fire on those who denied him hospitality (Luke 9:51–54); and he repeatedly emphasized charity, forbearance, and mercy, particularly in the Beatitudes (Matthew 5; Luke 6). In parables like the wheat and the tares (Matthew 13:24–43) and the Good Samaritan (Luke 10:25–37), tolerationists found humility about human knowledge and a call to ethical service of one's neighbors, rather than a triumphalist insistence on preserving "the" true religion. They also drew an ethic of Christian conduct toward their brethren from Paul's epistles. Paul had called on Christians to treat each other with moderation and humility (Philippians 4:5; 1 Timothy 1:13, 15); he further insisted that whatever is not of faith is sin and that faith is the gift of God rather than the result of human coercion (Romans 14:5, 23; 2 Corinthians 1:24). Paul's distinction between the carnal and spiritual realms (2 Corinthians 10:4; Ephesians 6:11–12) further strengthened tolerationists' arguments for separating political from ecclesiastical authority.

Yet for every tolerationist quoting a verse of Scripture in the fight against persecution, there was a defender of orthodoxy ready with a different one (or, perhaps, a competing interpretation of the same verse!). Antitolerationists pointed to the history of Israel as a clearly relevant example in which God himself had placed religious affairs under the broad purview of civil government. (Calvin's commentary on Isaiah, with its reference to monarchs as "nursing fathers" to Israel, viewed the magistrate's relationship to the church as one of "protection and defense.") They interpreted Jesus's silence on matters of government not as an implicit endorsement of religious liberty, but as deference to earthly authorities, a claim strengthened by Paul's injunction in Romans 13—"Be subject to the powers that be"—which appeared in countless works criticizing calls for toleration. Antitolerationists repeatedly asserted that toleration would sanction schism within the church and that this rupture of Christian unity would in turn lead to an onslaught of heresy, irreligion, and licentiousness.

Tolerationists, for their part, viewed persecution as violating both the proper relationship between individuals and God and the fundamental responsibility of individuals to work out their own salvation. In the words of William Penn, governments that decreed how God was and was not to be worshipped "directly invade divine prerogative, and divest the almighty of a due, proper to none besides himself [and enthrone] man as king over conscience." By contrast, the Anglican churchman and critic of toleration Samuel Parker insisted that "to exempt religion and the consciences of men from the authority of the supreme power is but to expose the peace of kingdoms to every wild and fanatick pretender, who may... under pretences of Reformation thwart and unsettle government without control." In many ways, these were less "arguments" between good-faith interlocutors than mutual recrimination events, conducted by parties beginning from fundamentally different premises talking past each other and assuming the worst of their opponents.

Calling these debates "Christian" does require some further clarification. The backdrop of much early modern tolerationism, particularly in England (and, later, America), lay in longstanding, virulent anti-Catholicism. Many committed tolerationists drew the line at tolerating Catholics, for what they took to be sound reasons. The papal bull *Regnan in Excelsis* (1570), which excommunicated Elizabeth I and encouraged Catholics to unseat her, provided English authorities with all the evidence they needed to cast Catholics in the most unfavorable light possible. From the Gunpowder Plot in 1605 to the 1641 Irish rebellion, which provided the justification for Cromwell's "pacification" campaign between 1649 and 1653, to the Protestant coup that unseated the tolerationist Catholic monarch James II in 1688, anti-Catholicism lay at the heart of English politics. It easily coexisted with a growing movement to tolerate Protestant Dissenters. Locke's exclusion of Catholics—as he obliquely put it, any church so constituted "that all those who enter into it do thereby ipso facto deliver themselves up to the protection and service of another prince" forfeits any claim to toleration—was anything but unique. Indeed, Protestant Dissenters in England sought to frame their Presbyterian and Anglican rivals as power-hungry analogues to Catholics, as in Milton's "New Presbyter is old priest writ large" or Penn's "Fly Rome at home!"

Psychological and epistemological arguments

Related to, but distinct from, the scriptural arguments was a set of arguments about the nature of belief in general, and of religious belief more specifically. Tolerationists insisted that belief was a faculty of human understanding, not will, and thus was impervious to coercion. In other words, what we believe is not under our voluntary control; governmental coercion or legal penalties can force people to behave (or not behave) in certain ways but are simply unable to compel their assent to particular articles of faith.

Alongside such a psychological, or epistemological, view about the nature of belief went a related claim that true religion lay within, in the realm of belief. Locke's *Letter Concerning Toleration* sums up these dual claims well:

> All the life and power of true religion consist in the inward and full persuasion of the mind.... And such is the nature of the understanding, that it cannot be compelled to the belief of anything by outward force. Confiscation of estate, imprisonment...nothing of that nature can...make men change the inward judgment that they have framed of things.

This emphasis on belief as the heart of religion is a particularly modern way of formulating such questions, and departed from traditions that emphasized the importance of ecclesiastical rituals and practices. But in combining claims about the nature of belief with the notion that true religion resides within, tolerationists considered themselves to have succeeded in placing force in matters of religion firmly beyond the pale as both illegitimate *and* ineffective, both un-Christian *and* doomed to fail.

Antitolerationists did not generally deny the claim that force was ineffective in producing belief. But in their minds, such an admission did not rule out the appropriateness of, say, compelling attendance at religious services, or outlawing certain types of religious gatherings, as a way of steering individuals away from erroneous or dangerous beliefs; or, conversely, of requiring them to hear godly preaching in an established church for the (potential) good of their souls. In other words, they argued, "internal" beliefs and "external" practices were not so clearly distinguishable as tolerationists would like to claim. Furthermore, if the nature of religion lay in internal belief, then to agitate for extensive freedom of worship or religious practice was unnecessary, since everyone already possessed freedom of belief; one could believe whatever one wished to believe, in the privacy of one's own mind. Toleration, by contrast, was a political issue, involving claims about governmental policy and public order, not merely the content of individual cognition. Hobbes's comments on miracles also apply to the politics of religion more generally: "A private man has always the liberty," Hobbes wrote in *Leviathan*, "(because thought is free) to believe, or not believe in his heart, those acts that have been given out for Miracles.... But when it comes to confession of that faith, the Private Reason must submit to the Publique." What tolerationists sought, in the eyes of their detractors, was not liberty of conscience, but rather liberty to engage in disruptive and illegal action under the pretense of religion—in other words, to cloak sedition as piety.

Historical and political arguments

One of the most significant challenges faced by early modern tolerationists was the perception that they were arguing for something fundamentally unprecedented—that rulers had always assumed responsibility not only for the physical security but also for the spiritual well-being of their people. In attempting to dispel the suspicions of their critics, advocates of toleration compiled copious historical catalogues listing episodes of peaceful coexistence between different religious groups and enumerating notable historical figures (monarchs and magistrates, theologians and ecclesiastical leaders) who had successfully managed religious diversity without resorting to persecution. Such works also, by contrast, put forward more ominous precedents, laying out the unhappy consequences suffered by persecuting regimes and rulers over time.

Tolerationists worked hard to establish their claim that, despite the frequent equation of religious dissent and political strife, it was not toleration but rather persecution that was responsible for civil unrest and armed conflict. As Castellio put it, in a sentiment later echoed by Locke and countless others, "Seditions arise from the attempt to force and kill heretics rather than from leaving them alone, because tyranny engenders sedition." In Locke's words: "It is not religion inspires [individuals to sedition]...but their sufferings and oppressions that make them willing to ease themselves."

Such a view, however, had to contend with the ubiquitous religious conflict that had engulfed Europe for much of the sixteenth and seventeenth centuries and the fact that it had, in reality, frequently been intertwined with armed uprisings and civil wars. English antitolerationists, for example, repeatedly railed about the close association between religious and political dissent, and the regicide of King Charles I in 1649 was never far from subsequent debates over toleration. As one author put it in a 1685 pamphlet:

> Has not...toleration, and liberty of conscience murdered one king, set up a thousand usurpers, made England suffer a thousand miseries, and cost this nation many thousand lives, many millions of treasure.... [W]hoever indulges those who plead conscience, opens, a secret sally-port to let in traitors disguised under the name of tender conscience.

Far from the high-minded aspiration of conscientious Christians, toleration was, to its detractors, an invitation to violent factionalism and anarchy.

Pragmatic, prosperity-based arguments

The passage of time and the persistence of dissent further encouraged the tolerationist view that governments' efforts were better spent managing the effects of religious diversity, in keeping the peace and safeguarding basic rights, than in attempting to punish religious dissenters. Many argued that toleration would promote civil peace, as groups with histories of conflict and hostility came to feel their prospects linked with those in other religious communities. Huguenot philosopher and controversialist Pierre Bayle argued that "one of the greatest wonders since the Edicts [of toleration] is that the people of France of different religions have lived in so much fraternity, notwithstanding that they have continually before them the histories of our civil wars." Such appeals often suggested that in fostering peace toleration would yield economic prosperity, that societies at war—with their neighbors or with themselves—were by definition weakened and prevented from reaching their full potential. Indeed, rulers often invited religious communities (such as Anabaptists in the German Palatinate) to settle in their territories as a way of repopulating areas devastated by war.

Appeals to the economic prosperity that purportedly accompanied toleration and civil and religious peace were widespread. English tolerationists often valorized the prosperous (tolerating) example of the Netherlands; Jean Bodin set his *Colloquium*—a conversation between individuals representing a number of different religious and philosophical traditions—in Venice, and that port city's cosmopolitan diversity and commercial vitality formed an important background to the work's praise of interreligious dialogue. It was no accident, on this view, that vibrant trading cities like Amsterdam or Antwerp were also places where religious diversity flourished.

This emerging pragmatic approach to toleration often relied on the notion of prudence, which involved distinguishing between what governments might wish to do and how a wise ruler would choose to proceed given practical realities on the ground. In his *Six Books of the Commonwealth*, Bodin echoed the views of French *politiques* like Michel de l'Hôpital, advancing toleration as a pragmatic tool for securing political order. Here again, theorists prioritized civil peace as an essential (perhaps *the* essential) function of government, calling on rulers to consider the interests of both prince and people and adopt a policy of toleration, particularly in situations where religious diversity had long been part of a community's makeup.

Part of this pragmatic defense of toleration involved supplementing philosophical arguments or scriptural citations with efforts to evoke horror and revulsion at the human cost of persecution. Servetus may have been burned at the stake in 1553, but more than a century later Bayle was still reminding readers of that event, pronouncing it "a horrid blot upon the earlier days of the Reformation." Quakers marshaled accounts of their persecution and used them in public appeals for relief, assembling extensive lists of maltreatment simply because of "our conscientious Dissent from the present church"; not only lurid punishments like jailing, fines, or whipping, but even "so much Goods… taken… that they had not a Cow left to give their young Children Milk." The Quaker Meeting for Sufferings eventually published two mammoth volumes elaborating the specific punishments levied on individuals and families, in an attempt to attract public sympathy for Dissenters' plight (and to bolster the spirits of those who continued to face persecution).

The combined force of these various arguments in favor of religious toleration—together with concrete developments like the publication of the Edict of Nantes; the Peace of Munster (1648), which established the Dutch Republic's independence; the Peace of Westphalia (also 1648), which ended the Thirty Years War and brought a measure of religious peace to Lutherans, Catholics, and Calvinists in the Holy Roman Empire and France; and the 1689 Toleration Act in England—proposed nothing less than a radical rethinking of both the role of civil government vis-à-vis religion and, conversely, the nature of religious community itself. Without jettisoning the longstanding biblical idea that government was necessitated by human fallenness and the need to restrain evildoers, tolerationists offered a view of government devoted not to enforcing orthodoxy but rather to balancing religious factions, protecting rights to gather and worship, and promoting the common good of the political community.

Locke's definition of a commonwealth, which he distinguished from the church, was just one such effort. He called it

> a society of men constituted only for the procuring, preserving, and advancing their own civil interests. Civil interests I call life, liberty, health, and indolency of body; and the possession of outward things, such as money, lands, houses, furniture, and the like. It is the duty of the civil magistrate... to secure unto all the people in general and to every one of his subjects in particular the just possession of these things belonging to this life.

Several decades earlier, in his *Bloudy Tenent of Persecution*, Roger Williams had referred to the church as "like unto a corporation, society, or company of East India or Turkey merchants": only when the health of the whole state is threatened by the activities of one of these "companies" is the magistrate justified in intervening in their affairs. (The health analogy was often quite literal: New England Puritan leader, and Williams's nemesis, John Cotton, analogized the banishment of heretics to excluding people with infectious diseases from society.) William Penn called on the English government to pursue a balance between the realm's three religious interests (Church of England, Roman Catholic, and Protestant Dissenter). For Bodin, a sovereign who took sides in a religiously divided society "abdicates his role of sovereign judge and becomes merely party leader."

Toleration in religion and beyond

The lives of Penn and Williams—whose English and American careers, separated by decades, nonetheless offer intriguing parallels—reinforce a particularly crucial point about toleration: it was never fixed in one place, but always simultaneously part of social processes in Europe and beyond, involving the movement of ideas, goods, and people. Colonial North America, from

THE

BLOVDY TENENT,

of PERSECUTION, for cauſe of CONSCIENCE, diſcuſſed, in

A Conference *betweene*

TRVTH and PEACE.

VVHO,

In all tender Affection, preſent to the High Court of *Parliament*, (as the *Reſult* of their *Diſcourſe*) theſe, (amongſt other *Paſſages*) of *higheſt conſideration*.

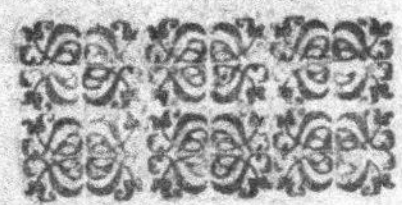

Printed in the Year 1644.

5. Roger Williams played a crucial role in the campaign for liberty of conscience both in England and in his role as founder of Rhode Island. *The Bloudy Tenent of Persecution* (London, 1644) offered his most extensive justification of toleration and liberty of conscience, arguing for a stark distinction between the church and the state.

New England to Georgia, was shaped by events in England and by European affairs more generally: the so-called Great Migration saw roughly 20,000 migrants journey to New England between 1620 and the mid-1640s; the English victory over the Dutch transferred a large swath of territory from Dutch to English hands in 1664; and further waves of settlers populated Pennsylvania during the 1680s. There were many reasons for these migrations, but aspirations for religious liberty played an important role. In such a vast territory, toleration frequently flourished on the ground due to the simple inability of would-be persecutors to impose uniformity.

Despite the best efforts of many of its participants, the Reformation produced not the triumph of truth over error but a pluralistic religious landscape and a transformed relationship between states and churches. Nowhere was toleration an easy achievement, and nowhere was its victory assured to last. In France, the Edict of Nantes endured for nearly a century before being revoked by Louis XIV in 1685, producing a flood of Huguenot refugees across Protestant Europe and further strengthening widespread Protestant rhetoric linking Catholicism to tyranny. The much-heralded achievement of toleration for English Dissenters in 1689 required a military invasion by a neighboring prince and the expulsion of a sitting monarch, and it was accompanied by a "Toleration Act" that never mentioned toleration and that protected neither Catholics nor those who denied the Trinity. That said, many tolerationists saw the act as a beginning: Locke described it as "not perhaps so wide in scope as might be wished for.... Still, it is something to have progressed so far."

Even while remaining firmly grounded in concerns about salvation, early modern toleration debates beckoned toward broader understandings of liberty. For John Milton, restrictions on publishing went hand in hand with restrictions on conscience, and in *Areopagitica* he noted the irony of those who had opposed

THE

GREAT CASE

OF

Liberty of Conſcience

Once more Briefly

Debated & Defended,

BY THE

Authority of *Reaſon, Scripture,* and *Antiquity*:

Which may ſerve the Place of a General Reply to ſuch late Diſcourſes, as have Oppos'd a Tolleration.

The Authour *W. P.*

For whatſoever ye would that men ſhould do unto you, that do you unto them, Matth. 7.22.
Render unto Cæſar, *the things that are* Cæſars; *and to* God, *the things that are* Gods, Matth. 12.27.

Printed in the Year, 1670.

6. In *The Great Case of Liberty of Conscience* (London, 1670), William Penn responded to attacks on toleration and presented his own theory of liberty of conscience, which he would attempt to put into practice more than a decade later in his colony of Pennsylvania.

ecclesiastical tyranny seeking to restrict the publication of books, since both "faith and knowledge thrives by exercise." In *The Great Case of Liberty of Conscience*, Penn argued that gathering with fellow believers was integral to the exercise of individual conscience and that liberty of conscience thus implied freedom of assembly; free speech and a free press were essential as well, since religious exercise involved preaching, proselytizing, and publishing defenses of Quaker principles. The centrality of this cluster of related rights—conscience, press, assembly, speech—at the heart of modern politics has been recognized by political theorists ever since.

Even more expansively, we might consider Benedict de Spinoza's recognition of the ubiquitous nature of human diversity, evident in his observation that "brains are as diverse as palates," and that the object of government is the free development of its people's minds and bodies. Spinoza thus concluded that "the best government will allow freedom of philosophical speculation no less than of religious belief." Pierre Bayle's tolerationist impulses similarly went beyond those of many of his contemporaries. While endorsing the idea that governments must preserve civil order and expressing customary suspicions of Catholicism, Bayle rejected many of the traditional justifications for limiting toleration. In his *Various Thoughts on the Occasion of a Comet* (1682), Bayle offered a kind of thought experiment about a "society of atheists," taking issue with a core claim of early modern toleration debates: that those who lacked belief in a Deity, and thus an afterlife, were inherently suspect on moral and ethical grounds. In criticizing such a view, Bayle offered examples of virtuous atheists from the classical world and insisted that professions of religion were not nearly as effective in discouraging vice as defenders of orthodoxy liked to think.

These incipient expansions from religion to other domains would ultimately provide toleration with a future far beyond anything early modern actors could have imagined. They also provided eighteenth- and nineteenth-century audiences with a foundation on which to build as they pushed for broader understandings of liberty, ones grounded in but transcending Reformation and early modern contexts. The arguments also traveled across the Atlantic, where Caribbean and American colonies reflected the contested nature of toleration. Puritan critics of the Anglican establishment, for example, pleaded for their own toleration, only to find themselves accused—by their own wayward son Roger Williams, and by their Quaker critics—of being no better than the Catholic persecutors that Protestants had faced during the Reformation. Williams's clarion call for toleration in both England and New England, put forward in his *Bloudy Tenent of Persecution*, established him as a transatlantic (if deeply controversial) voice for liberty of conscience.

Later in the seventeenth century, Penn's colonial undertaking in Pennsylvania provided Quakers—who had long faced persecution in England and elsewhere—a refuge where they could attempt to set up a godly society that would allow them to follow the dictates of their consciences. Toleration debates flourished in other North American and Caribbean colonies as well, where distance from metropolitan centers enabled a degree of flexibility and experimentation impossible in European settings.

Chapter 4
Enlightenment extensions and expansions

Debates over toleration in early modern Europe unfolded in different ways in different places, shaped by specific religious and political contexts. In England, the passage of the Toleration Act of 1689 settled one set of debates—whether religious dissent outside the established church would remain subject to persecution and legal penalties—but opened space for continued contestation over remaining civil restrictions (exclusion from positions in the universities or service in Parliament). Across the Channel, Montesquieu and Voltaire inherited the legacy of religious and political strife between a dominant French Catholic church and the Huguenot community, strife that stretched back to the sixteenth century and was reignited by Louis XIV's 1685 revocation of the Edict of Nantes. And the intertwined revolutionary struggles in eighteenth-century British North America and France ensured that philosophical debates over toleration remained deeply enmeshed in concrete political life.

In some places, advocates of toleration continued to rely on deeply religious arguments, either in line with the Christian foundations of early modern toleration or influenced by the increasingly prominent Deist movement—which affirmed a creative Deity but rejected much Christian orthodoxy—among elites. In others, the movement for liberty of conscience was accompanied by a deep-seated hostility to traditional religious authorities, who were perceived as threats to free inquiry, prosperity, and human happiness. (The two options—religious and anticlerical strategies and arguments—were by no means mutually exclusive.)

Toleration and the French Enlightenment

François-Marie Arouet, better known as Voltaire, was one of the most prominent thinkers of the French Enlightenment. Voltaire's interest in the subject of toleration was longstanding: a three-year sojourn in England had produced a volume of essays, *Letters on the English Nation* (1733), filled with observations about that realm's various sects and the broader politics of English religion. Voltaire emphasized the way that toleration contributed to social harmony and facilitated economic prosperity and the smooth functioning of commercial society. He wrote:

> Take a view of the Royal Exchange in London, a place more venerable than many courts of justice, where the representatives of all nations meet for the benefit of mankind. There the Jew, the Mahometan, and the Christian transact together, as though they all professed the same religion, and give the name of infidel to none but bankrupts. There the Presbyterian confides in the Anabaptist, and the Churchman depends on the Quaker's word.

Letters on the English Nation expressed effusive praise for the philosophy of Locke, the religious values of the Quakers, and the tolerationist efforts of William Penn in founding Pennsylvania. The work's implicit critique of French politics—where the revocation of the Edict of Nantes continued to deny basic rights to French Huguenots—led to its suppression by the French government and a warrant for its author's arrest.

Voltaire gave his most sustained attention to toleration in his 1763 *Traité sur Tolerance*. The *Treatise* was occasioned by the March 1762 execution of Jean Calas, a Toulouse Huguenot, for allegedly murdering his own son, purportedly to prevent him from converting to Catholicism. (In fact, Marc-Antoine likely committed suicide.) Despite an utter lack of evidence, rumors of Calas's involvement in his son's death spread quickly, and a Toulouse court sentenced him to a gruesome torture, after which he was promptly executed. Voltaire denounced the "superstitious and impulsive" mob that had called for Calas's execution, and the draconian sentence of the court, presenting Calas as a victim of fanaticism and irrational ignorance. More generally, Voltaire insisted on the power of reason to dissolve superstition and prejudice, and traced the bloody history of Christianity, drawing a stark contrast between it and the peaceful teachings of Jesus. Denying the widespread view that religious dissent sparks political rebellion, and echoing the views of Locke and others, Voltaire insisted that rebellion was the effect, not the cause, of persecution and intolerance, and pointed to numerous historical and contemporary examples where religious diversity had coexisted with civil peace and prosperity.

Voltaire insisted that neither he nor his *Treatise* were hostile to religion per se, and he admitted its salutary effect on morality: "Man has always needed a curb." He also insisted that a multiplicity of sects fostered civil peace: "The more sects there are, the less danger in each. Multiplicity weakens them." Such a view echoed those expressed earlier in the *Letters on the English Nation* and was shared by many of his eighteenth-century contemporaries, including Adam Smith and David Hume. (It also paralleled a broader analysis of faction put forward by Voltaire's contemporary Jean-Jacques Rousseau and, later, by James Madison in his tenth *Federalist* paper.) Voltaire framed the goal of toleration as ending persecution, preserving basic rights, and ensuring people's capacity to live their lives according to dictates of their consciences without fear of meeting the same fate as Jean Calas. Ultimately, in 1764, due in large part to Voltaire's efforts, Calas's conviction was posthumously annulled, and his family received an audience with King Louis XV as well as financial compensation from the Crown.

The *Treatise* was not Voltaire's last word on the subject, however. His *Philosophical Dictionary*, published a year later, contained an entry devoted to "Tolerance." Calling tolerance "the first law of nature," Voltaire referred to persecutors as "monsters." "We should pardon each other's errors," he wrote. "Discord is the great ill of mankind; and tolerance is the only remedy for it." He grounded this call for toleration on human fallibility: "We ought to be tolerant of one another, because we are all weak, inconsistent, liable to fickleness and error." Voltaire again stressed the peaceful potential of a multi-religious society, and pointed out the vast distance between the teachings of Jesus and the behavior of the church: The Christian "is without doubt the one which should inspire tolerance most, although up to now the Christians have been the most intolerant of all men." He blamed this fact on the fatal confluence of ecclesiastical and state power. In the course of just a few pages, this brief entry invoked virtually all of the classic defenses of toleration.

Like the *Treatise*, Voltaire's *Philosophical Dictionary* also became bound up with the religious and political conflict of his day. A young French nobleman, François-Jean Lefebvre de la Barre, was executed in 1766 in Abbeville, north of Paris, for blasphemy and sacrilege. Suspicion had fallen on de la Barre after the desecration of a crucifix and rumors that he and some friends had declined to salute a Catholic procession; a search of his rooms yielded (among other material) a copy of Voltaire's *Philosophical Dictionary*. De la Barre's torture and execution in July 1766 came with a twist: the *Dictionary* was ordered burned along with de la Barre's beheaded body (or, by one account, nailed to his torso). In contrast to the earlier Calas affair, however, Voltaire's efforts to clear de la Barre's name were less immediately successful, and the conviction stood until 1794, when it was reversed by the National Convention during the French Revolution.

Many of Voltaire's observations echoed those of his contemporary Charles Louis de Secondat, Baron de Montesquieu, whose

Spirit of the Laws (1748) was one of the eighteenth century's most far-reaching considerations of law, culture, and politics. Montesquieu's support for toleration was influenced by the example of predecessors like Bayle and Spinoza. Although, like most of his contemporaries, he assumed the superiority of Christianity over its competitors, Montesquieu admitted that "even a false religion is the best security we can have of the probity of men." He lamented interreligious conflict, since in his view religion "should never estrange man from a love and tenderness for his own species," and charged political authorities with safeguarding the public from strife between religions. Rulers should ensure that the religions within their territory "not only... not embroil the state, but... not raise disturbances amongst themselves." Montesquieu expressed caution about allowing new religions in societies where one was already established and dominant. Then again, where several religions were already in existence (an example that clearly applied to the situation in France), he recommended toleration, criticizing penal laws as ineffective and likely to alienate people from their rulers as well as their neighbors.

The significance of tolerance (or toleration) in eighteenth-century France is further evidenced by Jean-Edme Romilly's entry "Tolerance" in Diderot's *Encyclopedia* (1753). Observing that religion and conscience provoke the most frequent conflicts between people, Romilly directed his attention to "battling against the reign of prejudice." Like Voltaire, he grounded his defense of tolerance in the partiality and fallibility of human knowledge—each individual can know only a part of the truth, and we are all liable to be mistaken—as well as the inefficacy of violence and persecution to correct error: "Only evidence and reasoning can convince and persuade me." Romilly expressed confidence that truth, unaided, could overcome error and made clear that he did not view religious dissent as a cloak for sedition, asking "only for the liberty to think and profess the faith that they have judged the best, and who live in other respects as faithful subjects of the state."

The United States and France

The eighteenth-century revolutionary movements in the United States and France were shaped by each community's respective religious and political traditions, in which debates over toleration and conscience had long played important roles. The American revolutionaries inherited English notions of religious and political liberty as well as a religiously diverse colonial landscape, which had developed over the roughly century and a half that separated the first English colonization efforts from the outbreak of rebellion. In France, by contrast, the Catholic church enjoyed a close relationship with the monarchy, such that the increasing political upheaval was bound to hold dire consequences for religious institutions.

Thomas Jefferson's Bill for Establishing Religious Freedom, first submitted to the Virginia General Assembly in 1779, provided a kind of precis of the major tolerationist arguments of the day: that belief is impervious to physical coercion; that rulers are fallible and thus not appropriate or reliable as spiritual guides; that governments ought to restrict their concern to ensuring peace, prosperity, and the common good; that religious establishments corrupt religion; and that truth will triumph over error if only given the opportunity for free debate. All these arguments aimed to establish, in Jefferson's memorable phrase, that "our civil rights have no dependence on our religious opinions any more than our opinions in physics or geometry." Although it was not adopted until 1786 (and then in streamlined form), the bill displayed American leaders' familiarity with the Anglo-American legacy of debates over toleration and liberty of conscience. (This is not to say that the American founders were of one mind: John Adams endorsed the 1780 Massachusetts constitution, which provided public funds for Congregational churches.)

James Madison voiced similar tolerationist sentiments in his "Memorial and Remonstrance against Religious Assessments," which was signed by more than 1,000 Virginians and presented to the General Assembly in June 1785. Madison emphasized the "unalienable" nature of religious liberty, based on the overriding duty that each individual owed to the Creator. As such, religious establishments violated the basic tenets of Christianity (whose founder had, after all, insisted that his kingdom was not of this world). According to Madison, historical experience plainly showed that church establishments corrupted religion rather than advanced it. He also drew a slippery-slope argument, calling defenses of religious rights "prudent jealousy" to prevent future encroachments on other liberties. In making their arguments, thinkers like Madison and Jefferson moved beyond the language of toleration and often cited "natural rights," seeking to demarcate religion as an arena of human life over which the state held no legitimate authority.

When it came time to establish an American national government after the Revolution, the Constitutional Convention produced a document nearly silent on religion, with the exception of a prohibition on religious tests for officeholding (as still existed in Great Britain, for example). This silence caused concern among some of the Constitution's evangelical critics, who wished for a more robust recognition of God's mercies on their new nation. It did, however, accurately reflect the lack of a national religious consensus and the strength of various churches in different regions. The First Amendment to the Constitution—which initially limited the federal government only—forbade Congress from making any law "respecting an establishment of religion, or prohibiting the free exercise thereof." Its further provisions, forbidding Congress from abridging freedoms of speech, press, and peaceable assembly, provide a clear example of the way that the nation's founders understood this foundational cluster of liberties to lie at the heart of a free society.

In the early American context, the coalition that came together to defeat schemes for religious establishment included both religious skeptics and devout believers. Many skeptics worried about the potential for religious strife to bleed over into the governmental realm and would likely have agreed with Jefferson's famous dictum in Query 17 of *Notes on the State of Virginia* (1787): "The legitimate powers of government extend to such acts only as are injurious to others.... it does me no injury for my neighbour to say there are twenty gods, or no god. It neither picks my pocket nor breaks my leg." Others, like Massachusetts Baptist minister Isaac Backus, who served as a delegate to that state's constitutional ratification convention, were deeply pious Christians who worried about the effect of establishments on the purity of religion. Backus was the most prominent in a long line of Baptist theorists of religious liberty and advocates of church-state separation, frequently citing his Rhode Island predecessor Roger Williams, who had written in 1644 that the "unknowing zeal of Constantine and other Emperors did more hurt to Christ Jesus...than the raging fury of the most bloody Neroes."

The American hostility to established religion reflected a broader suspicion of centralized federal power, a legacy of the revolutionary struggle and a key element of the debate between Federalists and Anti-federalists (supporters and critics, respectively, of the proposed Constitution). On a more practical level, regional differences in the strength of various religious communities meant that no specific church was likely to command national support: Anglicans dominated in the South, Quakers and other Protestant denominations in the Middle Colonies, and Congregationalists in New England.

That said, even in the absence of a federal religious establishment, Christianity exercised enormous power over the lives of early Americans. Despite the effusive celebrations of figures like Washington and Jefferson—the first president had, after all, confidently proclaimed that the nation had moved "beyond toleration"—the early United States was characterized by an overwhelmingly Christian culture, and a host of restrictions on Catholics and non-Christians (which fell short of official ecclesiastical establishment, but restricted individual liberties nonetheless) prevailed well into the nation's second century. Christian missions and the nation's westward expansion, similarly, restricted the ability of indigenous Americans to freely exercise their own religions, to say nothing of their disastrous effects on indigenous life more generally. The restriction of central government power over religion preserved a particular species of liberty, to be sure, though it was no panacea for Protestant domination in its many forms, as American Mormons and other marginalized religious groups quickly found out. The triumphalist rhetoric of American liberty voiced by figures like Washington and Jefferson remained, at best, aspirational for many Americans.

Americans were hardly the only parties to revolution during the late eighteenth century. More than 100 years after Louis XIV's 1685 revocation of the Edict of Nantes, which signaled the end of basic toleration for French Protestants, Louis XVI granted a measure of toleration to Huguenots when he issued the Edict of Versailles in 1787. While hardly a full-blown bill of rights or guarantee of religious equality, the edict nonetheless removed the most onerous penalties on Protestant worship and safeguarded property rights and civil marriage.

On the momentous evening of August 4, 1789, when the National Constituent Assembly abolished aristocratic privileges, it also did away with the system of tithes that had supported the French Catholic church. Article 10 of the Declaration of the Rights of Man and the Citizen, adopted shortly thereafter, guaranteed that "No one may be disquieted for his opinions, even religious ones, provided that their manifestation does not trouble the public order established by the law." The years that followed saw increasingly vocal criticism of the Catholic church and an increasingly receptive attitude toward efforts to undermine the tight link between the French church and the French state. Given the close association between the monarchy and the church, it is not surprising that the progress of the revolution witnessed increasing hostility between political and religious authorities. Many leading figures in the revolutionary movement viewed the clergy as a counterrevolutionary force and church lands as a potentially lucrative source of revenue. The seizure of church lands and property in 1789 presaged the subordination of Catholic clergy to the state in the Civil Constitution of the Clergy a year later and increasingly harsh repression against priests throughout the 1790s. Alongside such attacks on the Catholic church went several ill-fated attempts to create a non-Christian cult, complete with its own rituals, festivals, and moral principles, that could unify rather than divide the nation. (Neither the Cult of Reason nor the Cult of the Supreme Being, which replaced it in 1794, garnered much popular support.)

The religious dimensions of these two revolutions were remarked upon by outside observers as well. Edmund Burke, who displayed far more sympathy with American revolutionaries than with their later French counterparts, described the Americans as embodying "the dissidence of dissent, and the Protestantism of the Protestant religion" in their zealous attachment to their English liberties. About the French revolutionaries, he was caustic and scathing, accusing them of having "plundered, degraded, and given [the clergy] over to mockery and scorn," and calling the French church "pillaged," as early as 1790. In his landmark work *Democracy in America* (1835), Alexis de Tocqueville contrasted the two revolutions by identifying a crucial convergence between "the spirit of religion and the spirit of liberty" in the American republic, as contrasted with European settings in which these two "spirits" often opposed one another; and, in an implicit contrast to his native land, stressed the social utility of American religion and its close connection to democratic institutions.

Mill, *On Liberty*

The cluster of related rights contained in the First Amendment to the United States Constitution, which protect religious exercise as well as speech, press, and assembly, illustrated how toleration went hand in hand with the emergence of more expansive understandings of human liberty. John Stuart Mill's *On Liberty* (1859) has been variously hailed as a vigorous defense of individuality and non-conformity—a new frontier in the history of toleration, if you will—and condemned for its division of the world into cultures ready for such freedom and others in which "the race itself may be considered as in its nonage." Nonetheless, in building upon the work of precursors like Milton and Locke while pressing for an expanded notion of individuality that went beyond toleration's religious foundations and paved the way for the pluralistic individualism characteristic of modern societies, *On Liberty* played an essential role in the ongoing conceptualization of toleration as a progressive value in the Western tradition.

Mill argued that, despite widespread lip service to concepts like conscience, religious freedom, and individuality, the power of social opinion, custom, and tradition remained formidable well into the nineteenth century. Such "social tyranny," he insisted, interfered with individual autonomy and prevented people from developing and pursuing their own ethical commitments just as powerfully—if not more so—than the overt persecution and violent intolerance of prior eras. In addition to defending an absolute liberty of thought and expression, Mill attempted to broaden the arenas in which freedom of action prevailed by introducing what he called "one very simple principle,"

> to govern absolutely the dealings of society with the individual in the way of compulsion and control, whether the means used be physical force in the form of legal penalties, or the moral coercion of public opinion. That principle is, that the sole end for which

> mankind are warranted, individually or collectively, in interfering with the liberty of action of any of their number, is self-protection. That the only purpose for which power can be rightfully exercised over any member of a civilized community, against his will, is to prevent harm to others. His own good, either physical or moral, is not a sufficient warrant.... The only part of the conduct of anyone, for which he is amenable to society, is that which concerns others. In the part which merely concerns himself, his independence is, of right, absolute. Over himself, over his own body and mind, the individual is sovereign.

Mill recognized the power of the psychological and social factors that motivate people to prohibit conduct that they find disagreeable: "so natural to mankind is intolerance in whatever they really care about," he wrote, "that religious freedom has hardly anywhere been practically realized." Mill called freedom of expression a "cognate liberty" to freedom of thought, and he viewed toleration of dissent as part of the collective search for truth (i.e., the fallibility argument, namely that the possibility of being mistaken makes persecution unacceptable). Mill's *On Liberty* thus echoed longstanding arguments for toleration and brought them squarely into nineteenth-century political debate.

But Mill sought to go farther, beyond the specific arenas of thought, discussion, speech, and press, and to advocate for the freedom of individuals to live their lives on their own terms. He offered a general argument against interference with individuals' life choices as part of a commitment to the development of individuality or, as he put it, "a character." Perhaps most relevant to our concerns is the way that Mill explicitly invoked the history of persecution and toleration and tied it directly to the changed circumstances of his time:

> The notion that it is one man's duty that another should be religious, was the foundation of all the religious persecutions ever perpetrated.... Though the feeling which breaks out in the repeated

> attempts to stop railway travelling on Sunday, in the resistance to the opening of Museums, and the like, has not the cruelty of the old persecutors, the state of mind indicated by it is fundamentally the same. It is a determination not to tolerate others in doing what is permitted by their religion, because it is not permitted by the persecutor's religion.

If European societies no longer imposed the most overt and violent forms of persecution, Mill claimed, they nonetheless countenanced a "social tyranny more formidable than many kinds of political oppression," one that promoted conformity and threatened individuals with ostracism for following their own understandings of how they ought to live their lives. Modern citizens should not comfort themselves with the assumption that persecution was gone for good, when such intolerance remained widespread.

The notion of "harm to others" remains difficult to define concretely in many instances; on further examination, Mill's "very simple principle" turns out to be anything but. Mill devoted an entire chapter of *On Liberty* to a less-than-successful attempt to specify the "limits to the authority of society over the individual," yet the harm principle has become one of the most enduring and debated concepts in modern political theory. (Saying that Mill's account has achieved a singular status in the canon does not mean it has lacked for critics: in *Liberty, Equality, Fraternity* [1873], Mill's contemporary James Fitzjames Stephen subjected it to a searing critique, viewing Mill's tolerance as little more than indifference and the harm principle as undermining any notion of community cohesion.) Contemporary theorists of toleration have attempted to clarify and expand the Millian harm principle so that it might speak to pressing twenty-first-century issues, including human rights, the family, environmental degradation, the economic sphere, and international relations. Such efforts to engage with Mill's theory about the appropriate limits of society's authority over the individual illustrate the continuing appeal of the "harm principle" to contemporary discussions of toleration.

Limits: Toleration and Anti-Catholicism

In the midst of ongoing movements in support of tolerationist ideals, one important exception continued to characterize the political landscape: support for toleration frequently coexisted with—indeed, was often integrally related to—anti-Catholicism. All theories of toleration contain limits—the "rejection component"—and for much of its modern history Catholicism (or, as Protestants often called it, "popery") has served as the quintessential example of the intolerable. Voltaire's *Treatise* had a great deal to say about Catholic intolerance and persecution but offered rather little by way of a substantive defense of French Protestantism. Denunciations of the Inquisition, which persisted into the nineteenth century, and Catholic religious orders more generally were routinely offered up by many Enlightenment thinkers, who saw them as a quintessential example of power-hungry church leaders attempting to create a "state within a state." (The same charge was occasionally leveled at European Jews as well, and the assimilationist pressures in much of the rhetoric around Jewish "emancipation" simultaneously offered religious toleration while undermining the unique legal protections that European Jewish communities had long enjoyed, even while they continued to face widespread social hostility.) In principles of toleration, such critics sought to weaken the Catholic church's influence and consequently to empower the state. Since the Inquisition targeted not only religious dissenters but also groups like the Freemasons and others deemed a threat to religious and political orthodoxy, many Enlightenment thinkers considered its overthrow essential to the advance of liberty more generally.

Even those accounts of American religious liberty that stress its promise and rapid spread acknowledge that it always harbored a deep strain of anti-Catholicism, and that many American Protestants considered the Catholic church a uniquely dangerous false religion. Such anti-Catholicism had traveled with English

Protestants to the American colonies during the seventeenth century and survived well into the founding era. In the debates over New York's 1777 constitution, no less prominent a founder than John Jay—who would go on to author several *Federalist* papers and serve as governor of New York, chief justice of the United States, and Secretary of State—proposed denying Catholics the free exercise of their religion unless they swore a renunciation of the pope's claims to political authority.

Anti-Catholicism showed itself to be a protean and enduring presence in toleration debates from the sixteenth through the twentieth centuries, during which countless thinkers framed Catholicism not only as an ecclesiastical rival to Protestant churches but also as a potentially tyrannical political influence within communities and in the international arena. Such Protestant anti-Catholicism is no mere antiquarian relic: just three months before the 1960 American presidential election, John F. Kennedy felt the need to appear before the Greater Houston Ministerial Association and proclaim his independence from the Vatican and his commitment to church-state separation.

Catholicism was hardly the only victim of American religious exclusion, and unlike indigenous religions, it was a familiar entity to American Protestants. By contrast, indigenous Americans often struggled to get local, state, and federal governments to recognize their rituals and ceremonies as "religious" at all; Christian policymakers and officeholders frequently either denied that they were religious or consigned them to the category of uncivilized "paganism."

Beyond toleration?

For a growing chorus of voices in the eighteenth century, toleration, though an important historical achievement, offered an insufficient measure of civil inclusion; they sought more expansive understandings of human liberty and broader civil freedoms beyond the narrowly religious sphere. The perception that toleration was inherently limited and unduly minimal, and that terms like religious liberty or liberty of conscience were more appropriate for modern times, not only motivated Washington's 1790 letter to the Newport Jewish congregation but made its way into works by prominent philosophers and polemicists.

In his noted essay "What is Enlightenment?" (1784), Immanuel Kant analogized the process of enlightenment to humanity emerging into rational adulthood out of "self-imposed immaturity." Kant called for humans to "Dare to know!" and to reject claims of superior knowledge put forward by ecclesiastical, political, and educational authorities. Urging rulers to "repudiate[e] the arrogant word 'tolerant,'" Kant praised Prussian monarch Frederick the Great for leaving his subjects "complete freedom... in religious matters." While acknowledging that "it is still far from true that men are... capable of using their own reason in religious matters," Kant insisted that "we live in an age of enlightenment."

Similar sentiments were expressed by the transatlantic revolutionary Thomas Paine, whose 1791 *Rights of Man* praised the French Constitution for renouncing "toleration, and intolerance also," instead establishing "universal right to conscience." Like Washington, Paine denounced toleration as an "act of assumed authority," despotic in its claims that some humans have the right to dictate the terms by which others will discharge their duties to God. Locating the core of religion in "man bringing to his Maker the fruits of his heart," Paine insisted that all religions are "in their nature mild and benign, and united with principles of morality." When conjoined with the state, however, religions often lose "their native mildness, and become morose and intolerant." Not only did the intertwining of religious and political authority pervert true religion; it also damaged the prosperity and unity of the state.

In addition to moving beyond a metaphor so steeped in notions of minimalistic dissent and grudging permission, and compatible with continuing modes of exclusion, these attempts to move beyond toleration also shifted their focus from narrowly religious questions to the more expansive realms of free inquiry and ethical life. Kant's "What is Enlightenment?" addressed not only religion but also education and freedom of expression; in *On Liberty*, as we have seen, Mill connected free thought and expression to non-conformity and the development of individual character.

This push beyond mere toleration was neither quickly nor easily accomplished. To take just one example, vestiges of Anglican supremacy in England were slow to fall, even after the attainment of basic toleration in 1689. Concerted social movements were needed to guarantee further degrees of inclusion in public life for religious minorities. Although the Toleration Act provided a safe space within the public realm for Dissenters, not until well into the nineteenth century did Parliament finally repeal the Test Act, which had prevented most non-Anglicans from serving in public office by mandating attendance at Anglican churches and disavowal of Catholic doctrine. The Sacramental Test Act (1828) repealed the requirement that government officials receive the Eucharist in the Church of England; the Catholic Relief Act (1829) permitted Catholics to serve in Parliament; the Jews Relief Act (1858) permitted Jews to remove the phrase "upon the true faith of a Christian" from the oath of office, and thus to serve in Parliament.

But the gradual process of inclusion would require even further steps. The Oaths Act (1888), passed thanks to the efforts of atheist activist Charles Bradlaugh, permitted the substitution of affirmations for all required oaths. The Universities Test Act of 1871 removed religious tests for university positions at the major English universities. (Although a system of Dissenting academies had existed since the seventeenth century to offer educational opportunities for the realm's non-Anglicans, Dissenters' inability to study or obtain posts in the country's major centers of learning and social influence represented yet another way in which toleration coexisted with exclusion.) Individuals had not been, strictly speaking, "persecuted" by being excluded from the universities or denied the opportunity to serve in Parliament. They had, however, been denied full participation in public life on account of their religious commitments, and the growing sentiment for repeal involved, at the least, a growing recognition that such civil disabilities were morally and politically consequential.

Chapter 5
Colonial and imperial complications

Although debates about toleration grew in political influence and philosophical sophistication during the early modern and Enlightenment eras, they were never confined to those regions commonly known as Christendom. Hand in hand with developments in Europe and the nascent United States went a parallel, intertwined process of colonization and imperialism, by which European ideas and practices—philosophical, theological, political, economic—became enmeshed in global processes of rule and domination. As toleration developed into a foundational element of the emerging liberal democratic tradition, it was increasingly implicated in the colonial and imperial projects undertaken by many of those European states, from French, English, and Spanish efforts in the Americas and the Caribbean to broader European interventions in Asia, Africa, and Oceania. Events in Europe and in its colonies were always part of a common process of negotiation, mobilization, and contestation, by which societies (in the metropole and on the peripheries) grappled with a series of controversies driven by questions of toleration: Who or what types of groups, beliefs, or behaviors should be permitted? On what grounds? Toward what ends? Toleration thus served not merely as a philosophical abstraction or a political practice with European or American ramifications, but as a tool of empire and global control.

The term “empire” itself requires some clarification, as European states pursued varying paths in their attempts to control their overseas territories. In the English case, earlier colonial enterprises (in Ireland, the Caribbean, and North America) achieved a kind of organizational maturity with the formation of the Lords of Trade and Plantations in 1675 and, later, the Board of Trade. Other European actors—Dutch, French, Portuguese, German—conducted their imperial and colonial ventures in different ways, with some emphasizing the control of trade and others planting settled colonies, and all to some degree or another driven by missionary ideals. The result sought was always the same: to gain economic advantage and political control, and to facilitate European “civilizing” missions and/or the conversion of natives to Christianity (and, in some places, extermination of native populations altogether). European settlers and the governments and companies that sponsored them often employed the rhetoric of toleration while imposing draconian controls on indigenous peoples; toleration was closely connected with the subjugation of native populations.

In pursuit of these various goals, European powers often viewed toleration as crucial to their success in attracting settlers or investment to distant locations or securing civil peace over potentially restive populations. In fact, William Penn’s first written defense of toleration—nearly fifteen years before the founding of Pennsylvania—appealed to a key colonial administrator in Cork to realize that persecution constituted “a bad argument to invite English hither” (to Ireland). The aspiration to escape persecution (along with a host of other motivations, to be sure) fired American colonization from New England and Pennsylvania to Maryland and Carolina. Nor did the Dutch escape the common need to balance standards of traditional religious authority with the enticement of settlers to their colonial lands: promises of toleration were crucial to the settlement of Dutch Brazil and New Netherland.

Spain and the Iberian colonies

Muhammad XII's 1492 surrender of Granada to Ferdinand and Isabella, the Catholic Monarchs of Spain, completed the Spanish Reconquista and extinguished Muslim control in the Iberian peninsula. The surrender of Granada would be catastrophic for non-Christians: the Alhambra Decree of March 1492 banished Jews from Spain, while Spanish Muslims faced an increasingly strict policy of forced conversions over the next two decades. Even conversion was no guarantee of safety: Muslim converts ("Moriscos") continued to face suspicion, marginalization, prosecution, and at times expulsion, as authorities often doubted the sincerity of their conversions and considered them a potential fifth column with Ottoman sympathies. Similar suspicions dogged "Conversos," Jews who had converted to Christianity, many of whom continued to maintain Jewish traditions discreetly.

Just a month after the Alhambra Decree, the Spanish monarchs issued a commission to the Genoese explorer Christopher Columbus for a voyage to the west. These measures—commissioning Columbus and attempting to eradicate Spain's Jewish and Muslim communities—along with the later establishment of a tribunal of the Spanish Inquisition in Granada in 1526, set in motion an expansive imperial undertaking that would vie with Protestant powers to the north and the Ottoman Empire in North Africa and the Mediterranean. The spread of the Spanish Empire across the Atlantic Ocean to the Caribbean, Mexico, and the Americas and eventually into the Pacific; the incursions of the *conquistadores*, with their genocidal consequences for indigenous populations; and the impact of gold and sugar on transatlantic economies: such developments illuminate questions of imperial religious policy, and they shed important light on the interplay between empire and toleration.

The development of empire not only involved Spain in the struggle to assert control over indigenous peoples and new lands; it also involved the kingdom in rivalry, conflict, and competition with other European powers. Protestant nations, particularly the English, engaged in a robust effort to distinguish themselves from their (Catholic) Spanish rivals by making exaggerated and hyperbolic claims about Spanish persecution and intolerance. Although the term was not coined until the early twentieth century, the "Black Legend" (*leyenda negra*) referred to an age-old phenomenon: a (Protestant) effort to portray Spanish colonization as uniquely horrific compared with that of other European states. The Black Legend emphasized Spanish cruelty, perfidy, and violence as opposed to other nations' purportedly gentler behavior in their colonial exploits and added lurid tales of greed, bigotry, and gratuitous savagery to standard anti-Catholic claims about Spanish religious intolerance.

What gave the Black Legend its power among Protestant audiences was not simply its contribution to the self-serving and self-congratulatory lore of Protestant liberty (including religious liberty), but that it often drew on Spaniards' own tales of the gruesome and callous behavior of their compatriots. Most notable among such accounts was surely Bartolomé de las Casas's *Short Account of the Destruction of the Indies*, first published in the early 1550s. Las Casas was a reformer at heart and hoped that his reporting of the abuses he witnessed would spur Spanish authorities to reform colonial practices. Such hopes proved to be misguided, but the rapid translation and publication of his text in Dutch and English show just how useful las Casas's detailed attack on Spanish imperial violence could be to those seeking to brand a Catholic power as uniquely intolerant and savage. (The Black Legend would persist into the nineteenth and even twentieth centuries, providing a potent propaganda tool for framing conflicts as diverse as the Mexican War, the Spanish-American War, and the California gold rush; in other

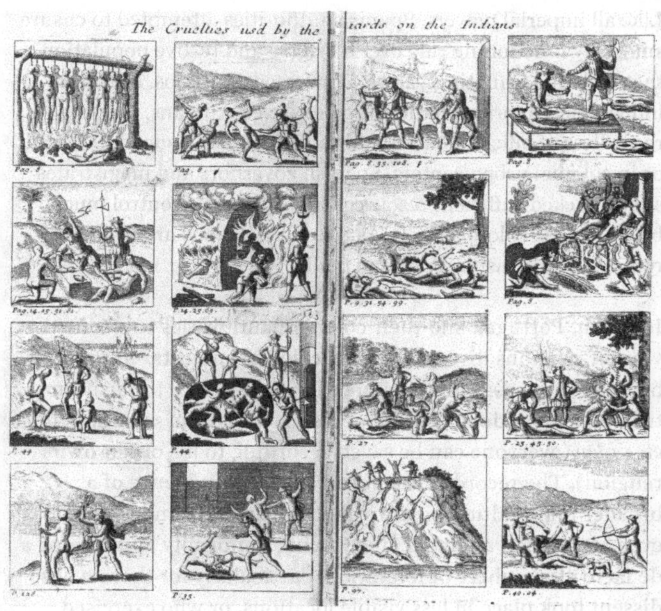

7. In the sixteenth century, the Spanish clergyman Bartolomé de las Casas published *A Brief Account of the Destruction of the Indies*, detailing the cruel treatment that the Spaniards inflicted on the indigenous populations of the Americas. This illustration is taken from an English edition of las Casas, *An account of the first voyages and discoveries made by the Spaniards in America: containing the most exact relation hitherto publish'd, of their unparallel'd cruelties on the Indians*. . . .

words, anywhere Protestants faced Catholics in close and competitive quarters, and saw value in depicting them as distinctly cruel and untrustworthy.) Not unlike the notion of an Iberian *convivencia*, the image of peaceful coexistence of Jews, Christians, and Muslims during the medieval era, the Black Legend's importance lay more in its power as political rhetoric than as a factual account of the behavior of Spanish authorities, either in their own right or vis-à-vis other European colonizers.

Like all imperial powers, Spanish authorities attempted to ensure smoothly functioning rule over a diverse and restive population that included Christians, Jews, Conversos, Moriscos, Muslims, indigenous American natives, and enslaved Africans. But regardless of official policies and proclamations issued in Madrid or in colonial urban centers, Spanish governors and magistrates simply lacked sufficient resources to secure their control much beyond those colonial cities. As a result, religious uniformity remained more aspiration than reality.

In Spain, Portugal, and their colonies, authorities confronted vibrant religious diversity among colonial subjects, epitomized by numerous cases of individuals brought before Inquisition tribunals for endorsing statements like *cada uno se puede salvar en su ley* (everyone can be saved according to his or her own religion). The records of such cases provide evidence of a broader multicultural context that consistently undermined even attenuated attempts at enforcing uniformity and created a de facto atmosphere of toleration, particularly for those whose dissent took place in less visible locations, or who exercised discretion in their behavior. After all, if the Inquisition ultimately failed to stamp out dissent across Europe, it was even less likely to have success in remote locations like New Spain. Circumspect Conversos were often able to practice their religion, including syncretic practices that drew on their Jewish heritage, far from the watchful eye of Inquisition officials, aided by their centrality to New Spain's economy and officials' corresponding reluctance to take action against them. The same could be said for the colony of Brazil, which also appealed to so-called "New Christians" seeking a life at some remove from Portuguese surveillance and control. The reality of life in the colonies, or on the frontier, often bore little resemblance to that decreed by colonial authorities, and a religious vibrancy operated just below the surface of official orthodoxy.

British India

In contrast to seventeenth-century toleration debates in England and the American Revolution and founding, in which the participants shared common bonds of language, religion, and history, British control over the Indian subcontinent brought Europeans into close proximity with cultural and religious forms at least unfamiliar, and at most anathema, to the colonizers. Toleration would play a key role in the process by which British colonial authorities made sense of, and responded to, those unfamiliar surroundings.

British involvement in India long predated the eighteenth century, and questions of toleration were never far from the surface. The 1661 treaty by which Portugal ceded Bombay to England (part of Catherine of Braganza's dowry upon her marriage to King Charles II of England) included guarantees of religious observance for Catholics there. Early on, the East India Company's main concern was facilitating smooth and stable trading relations in an environment where the British were vastly outnumbered. The company thus adopted a policy of non-interference with local religious customs, even going so far as to endow and protect Hindu institutions, collect taxes for the maintenance of shrines and temples, and oversee religious festivals. In their pursuit of social (and commercial) harmony, company officials sought to keep Christian missionaries out of India, fearful of the divisive effect they were sure to have on inter-communal relations.

The period between Governor-General Warren Hastings's Judicial Plan of 1772 and Queen Victoria's Proclamation of 1858, which imposed direct rule by the Crown, illustrates the important role played by toleration in the dynamics of imperial rule. Among other things (chiefly, standardizing tax collections and putting the company's financial affairs in order), Hastings's Judicial Plan established a system of civil courts, in which Muslim and Hindu communities maintained authority over internal matters such as marriage and inheritance. The company also sought to play the role of benevolent overseer ensuring freedom of religion for Indian Hindus as well as their Muslim (Mughal) rulers. In order to tolerate Hinduism, the British had to identify it, and doing so posed challenges not found in Europe, where toleration debates generally operated in a context of Catholic-Protestant relations. Though reviled by many in England, Catholicism was at least recognizable; Indian religious practices were another matter entirely.

Crucial to the process of naming and sorting out the diverse communities that made up Indian society was the *Code of Gentoo Laws*, commissioned by Hastings in 1773, assembled by Brahmin scholars working for (and paid by) the Governor-General, and published in 1776. (The now-archaic term "Gentoo" was frequently used by early modern Europeans to refer to the inhabitants of South Asia, whereas "Hindu" became increasingly prominent during this period and was useful for distinguishing between Muslim and non-Muslim South Asians.) Nathaniel Halhed's translator's preface to the *Code*—Halhed translated the work from Persian into English—connected toleration with imperial goals, highlighting "the importance of the commerce of India" to the British Empire and noting the key goals of securing Indians' affections and guaranteeing the territories' stability: "Nothing can so favourably conduce to these two points as a well-timed toleration in matters of religion." The *Code* invoked Roman toleration and presented Hinduism as a venerable religious tradition, with its own scriptures and clerical elites (Brahmins) who oversaw communal life. (The degree to which imperial officials "invented" Hinduism, in an attempt to render it governable through the European category of "religion," continues to stoke controversy.)

Among the East India Company's directors, the notion of Hinduism as a coherent, if erroneous, religious tradition,

A

C O D E

O F

GENTOO LAWS,

O R,

ORDINATIONS

OF THE

PUNDITS,

FROM A

PERSIAN TRANSLATION,

MADE FROM THE

ORIGINAL,

WRITTEN IN THE

SHANSCRIT LANGUAGE.

LONDON:

PRINTED in the YEAR M DCC LXXVI.

8. ***A Code of Gentoo Laws*, a key element of the British effort to identify the core tenets of Hindu law and culture, was produced in 1776 by a panel of Brahmin scholars commissioned by Governor-General Warren Hastings. The work was translated into English by philologist Nathaniel Brassey Halhed.**

deserving of the protection afforded by toleration, went hand in hand with a reluctance to allow Christian missionaries into India. Toleration, on this understanding, related less to an individual, conscience-based right to worship and more to the capacity of communities (in this case, Indian Hindus) to live according to their customs and traditions, and to organize their common lives according to those traditions without the interference of powerful and disruptive rivals.

India was not the only arena that the company had to navigate, however. It also functioned in a domestic English context, one characterized by proselytization pressures from a number of groups, including the Anglican-dominated Society for the Promotion of Christian Knowledge (SPCK) and the Protestant Society for the Protection of Religious Liberty, in which Dissenters and an increasingly influential evangelical movement were heavily represented. Evangelical voices loudly proclaimed Hinduism a false religion, the toleration of which simultaneously threatened Indians' immortal souls and violated Christians' freedom to proselytize. Charles Grant's *Observations on the State of Society among the Asiatic Subjects of Great Britain*—Grant was a prominent evangelical Member of Parliament who would become the East India Company's chairman in 1805—denounced Hinduism as a religion that imposed barbaric customs on its adherents and kept them in spiritual darkness. While disavowing any intent to violate Indians' rights—"Toleration in matters of religion is well understood," he proclaimed, and "Religion is not propagated by force"—Grant urged that Christian missionaries be allowed into India. "All that is now proposed," he insisted, is "that . . . individuals, armed with nothing but truth, reason, and argument, shall in a mild, pacific way, communicate the Christian system to those who have never hitherto had an opportunity of hearing it." Rather than coercion, "the ultimate object is moral improvement." (The claim that English missionaries in India were armed with "nothing but truth, reason, and argument" illustrates the almost-willful blindness to the realities of power that often accompanied these arguments over toleration.)

Negative publicity about corruption in the East India Company provided an opportunity for evangelicals to mount a massive public campaign, seeking to insert a clause requiring missionary access, when the Company's charter came up for renewal in 1793. Prominent evangelicals like Grant and abolitionist William Wilberforce were at the forefront of this campaign. The company successfully resisted evangelical pressure, but it could not hold out indefinitely.

The company's charter came up for renewal again in 1813. Wilberforce denounced Hinduism in terms that evoked earlier English attacks on Catholicism: "We find the morals and manners of the natives of India just such as we might have been led to expect from a knowledge of the dark and degrading superstitions, as well as of the political bondage, under which they have been so long bowed down." Though they disavowed "intolerant interference" with Indians, the Protestant Society for the Protection of Religious Liberty voiced its "anguish and... horror [at] the moral depression and religious ignorance of very many millions of immortal beings, who people the plains of India." As such, the Society viewed "the power possessed and exercised by the East-India Company to prohibit Christian Missionaries from... the vast dominions under their control, as the greatest impediment... to the progress of Christianity in India." A "pious clause" expressing concern for Indians' "religious and moral improvement" and ensuring access for "persons desirous of going to... India, for the purpose of accomplishing... benevolent designs" while guaranteeing "the natives of India... the free exercise of their religion," became part of the company's 1813 charter.

Toleration figured into British imperial conduct not only with regard to allowing Christians access to the Indian mission field, or safeguarding an ostensibly ancient religion from outside interference. It also arose in dealing with ritual practices that evoked outrage among many observers. Despite a growing clamor against it in England, the Hindu practice of *sati* (the ritual burning of a widow on her deceased husband's funeral pyre) was tolerated by British authorities in India well into the nineteenth century.

The policy turned on a much larger inquiry: what was religion, and what sorts of behavior should be included under the umbrella of religious toleration? Such debates took place against the backdrop of European notions of what "religion" looked like, how it operated, and what relationship it ought to have with the state. So long as *sati* could be grounded in Hindu sacred texts, and framed as widows' voluntary acts of pious devotion, imperial officials viewed it as religious (if distasteful, to say the least), and thus protected by British tolerationist commitments. Even in 1829, when Governor General Lord William Bentnick finally outlawed *sati*, he insisted that his decision did not stem from Christian missionary impulses. His justification failed to convince many Hindus; a January 1830 "Petition of the Orthodox Hindu community of Calcutta" denounced Bentnick's action as "an unjust and intolerant dictation in matters of conscience." Notable here is the way that a combination of the British tradition of toleration and British imperial control drove Hindu elites to use the vocabulary of conscience and toleration in their attempts to safeguard their distinctive cultural practices.

In fact, some participants in the British argument over *sati* went so far as to quote Locke's *Letter Concerning Toleration* to justify their positions in favor of its suppression. A paper published in the March 1821 *Friend of India* reminded readers that Locke had always distinguished between "speculative opinions," which deserved toleration, and things that were "not lawful in the ordinary course of life, nor in any private house, and therefore neither are they so in the worship of God." It was self-evident to the author of this paper that *sati* fell into the latter category, as little more than a barbaric custom with some "religious" window-dressing, and that efforts to abolish it posed no danger to authentic religion and the British commitment to toleration.

The Indian Rebellion of 1857, which led to the passage of the Government of India Act and the Crown's assumption of direct sovereignty, again brought toleration into debates over colonial policy. Under-secretary of the Home Department William Massey gave a speech on India noteworthy enough to garner a rebuke from John Stuart Mill, via a footnote in Mill's *On Liberty*. (Mill himself was deeply involved in East India Company business, serving in various company posts over more than three decades.) Like Grant and other evangelical activists who preceded him, Massey drew a stark line between tolerating different groups of Christians and tolerating Hinduism. Massey called the "freedom of worship among Christians who worshipped on the same foundation... the great corner stone of the religious liberties of this country [England]," but quickly added that "to apply the word toleration to a people who worshipped miserable and bloodstained idols" represented "a gross abuse of the term." Furthermore, he charged the "toleration of... the superstition which they called religion" with "retarding the ascendancy of the British name and preventing the salutary growth of Christianity."

Mill's response was biting. He decried Massey's remarks as highlighting the precarity of toleration even in the "enlightened" nineteenth century. What some would describe as a revival of religion in British society, Mill averred, was little more than "the revival of bigotry," and where bigotry was, intolerance and persecution could never be far behind. He lamented the fact that "a man who has been deemed fit to fill a high office in the government of this country... maintains the doctrine that all who do not believe in the divinity of Christ are beyond the pale of toleration." "Who, after this imbecile display," Mill asked, "can indulge the illusion that religious persecution has passed away, never to return?"

This argument highlights a key point regarding toleration. Whatever else they might reflect—requirement of true Christianity, prudential accommodation to local circumstances, recipe for smooth trading relations—arguments over toleration were always, simultaneously, arguments about power. The language of toleration (its categories, justifications, background assumptions, and limits) was integral to the extension of British imperial power over the Indian populace and economy. And once in place, it framed a wide range of issues like proselytization, ritual, communal practice, and intercommunal relations. The British national self-image, of itself as a tolerating nation, coexisted smoothly with power politics and imperial control. Indeed, even as she was seizing control of India from the East India Company, Queen Victoria denied any interest in "impos[ing] our convictions on any of our subjects" and disclaimed "all interference with the religious belief or worship of any of our subjects."

Such questions continued to resonate into the twentieth century, in controversies over groups like Arya Samaj, a proselytizing Hindu movement, and in Gandhi's criticism of proselytization as threatening social peace and ultimately disrespecting the commitments held by members of India's religious communities. Gandhi claimed that proselytization "will mean no peace in the world." Despite being characterized by some as "striving for tolerance," Gandhi actually displayed a great deal of ambivalence about the concept. He distinguished between two potential positions: "mutual toleration" and "equality of all religions," casting his lot with the latter. "We must have innate respect for other religions as we have for our own... not mutual toleration, but equal respect." Elsewhere, after admitting that "I do not like the word tolerance, but could not think of a better one," Gandhi contended, "Tolerance implies a gratuitous assumption of the inferiority of other faiths to one's own." A more satisfactory approach, in his view, "teaches us to entertain the same respect for the religious faiths of others as we accord to our own."

9. Mohandas Gandhi (right) and Muhammad Ali Jinnah, head of the All-India Muslim League and founder of Pakistan, meet in Bombay in 1944. Gandhi's call for interreligious harmony proved unable to prevent the partition of British India into two separate nations, India and Pakistan, at independence in 1947.

And yet notwithstanding his preference for equal respect between religions, facilitated by his notions of an "underlying unity" among them all—the world's religions are like "beautiful flowers from the same garden"—Gandhi at times expressed hope for a notion of tolerance that "does not mean indifference towards one's own faith, but a more intelligent and purer love for it.... Cultivation of tolerance for other faiths will impart to us a truer understanding of our own." Late in life, Gandhi traced his own trajectory in terms that evoke the contrast between toleration and equality: "I have, of course, always believed in the principle of religious tolerance. But I have even gone further. I have advanced from tolerance to equal respect for all religions."

This history continues to influence Indian religious and political argument, including the recent resurgence of Hindu nationalism, which asserts India's fundamentally Hindu nature, casts Muslims and Christians as interlopers, and often sanctions violence toward Muslims.

Christianity, toleration, and slavery

Among the arguments advanced during the formative early modern toleration debates was the idea not only of a fundamental right to gather for worship, but a broader Christian duty to evangelize. Such a view of Christianity often relied on the Great Commission, in which Jesus charged his disciples to "go and make disciples of all nations" (Matthew 28:16–20). Preaching and conversion have always played a prominent role in the Christian tradition, and the Christian tradition has played a prominent role in the history of toleration. But the notion of Christianity as an inherently proselytizing and universalistic religion, seeking the salvation of all, which figured prominently in the debates over allowing Christian missionaries into India, had its limits, and slave societies often made those limits clear.

European toleration coexisted with colonial and imperial relations grounded in the domination of non-European populations. It also coexisted with Atlantic slavery. Slavery in places like Virginia and the Caribbean is a familiar topic, but even where a reputation for robust toleration existed, as in the Middle Colonies, the slave system fit neatly alongside expansive protections for religious practice. The 1665 "Concession and Agreement of... New Jersey" promised that "no person... shall be any ways molested, punished, disquieted or called in question for any difference in opinion or practice in matter of religious concernments," and guaranteed all residents the right to "freely and fully... enjoy... their judgments and consciences in matters of religion." It also contained incentives for settlers to bring slaves with them when they settled in the colony. (The 1669 Fundamental Constitutions of Carolina offered similar guarantees.) This simultaneous protection of religious freedom and slavery—guaranteeing one species of liberty while at the same time rewarding the deprivation of another—illustrates with stark clarity one of the enduring paradoxes of American history.

Although Quakers were integral to the attainment of early modern toleration, many prominent Friends participated in the slave trade, abetted by the interconnected nature of the North American and Caribbean economies. During the eighteenth and nineteenth centuries, Quakers developed a consistent and coherent witness against slavery, and the history of abolition in the United States can hardly be written without an acknowledgment of their important role. But seventeenth-century Quakerism was another matter, and few during those years saw any contradiction between an embrace of spiritual liberty, the vaunted Quaker "Peace Testimony," and a commitment to toleration and liberty of conscience on the one hand, and the ownership of human beings on the other.

Conversion, toleration, enslavement, and freedom existed side by side in the world of Atlantic slavery. In Barbados, for example, slaveholders' resistance to proselytization of their enslaved population was based in large part on unease about enslaving fellow Christians and concern that conversion would lead to calls for emancipation. The English Parliament, Dutch colonial officials, and religious leaders like the Quaker George Fox (whose visit to Barbados in 1672 yielded an impassioned plea for slaveowners to attend to the spiritual condition of their property, but not a systemic critique of slavery itself) and later the evangelical George Whitefield could deal with questions of evangelism and the conversion of enslaved individuals at a remove, framing them as obligations of paternalistic Christian conduct. Slaveowners themselves, however, took a much dimmer view. Their hostility to conversion and the religious instruction of their slaves lay in the fear that Christian notions of spiritual liberty would threaten the willingness of the enslaved to submit themselves to slaveowners' authority. Would slaves who converted to Christianity take Galatians 3:28—"There is neither Jew nor

Gentile, neither slave nor free, nor is there male and female, for you are all one in Christ Jesus"—to heart? Would they refuse to work on the Sabbath? The emergence of race as a categorical distinction between freedom and enslavement—in other words, the replacement of "Christian" by "white" as the legal and cultural category associated with freedom—made Christianity safe for slavery and ensured that religious freedom, such as it was, did not encroach into other domains or threaten the economic interests of slaveholders.

Toleration debates played an important role in European colonial and imperial projects. The necessities of administering complex organizations of people, goods, and services over vast distances often led to de facto toleration "on the ground" with regard to religion. Alongside such toleration, attempts to subjugate indigenous populations, often in stark and violent ways, remained constant. Christian hegemony served as a constant backdrop in these contexts as well, as in evangelical efforts to obtain missionary access to India and the (only ever partially successful) Inquisition efforts to stamp out dissent. In this sense, Christianity represented a limiting factor that was always waiting in the wings to impose orthodoxy on diverse indigenous populations and/or Europeans who traveled to those lands. The figure of Wilberforce—whose career exhibited both religious bigotry and vigorous campaigning against the slave trade—illustrates some of these paradoxes of toleration in practice. The twentieth century would test the capacity of toleration's historical arguments to speak to new and radically transformed realities.

Chapter 6
Contesting and defending toleration

Toleration's critics and defenders continue to debate its merits. A series of recent controversies and critical engagements have assured the idea of "tolerance"—defined in a variety of ways, all of them related to the tolerationist legacy—a heightened public profile in many liberal democracies. Such a profile has often appeared in connection with controversies over "multiculturalism" or the challenges posed by globalization, or the resurgence of ethnicity and religious fundamentalism(s) in a range of arenas from the Iranian Revolution to the post-Soviet rise of Islamism in Central Asia. The history and politics of toleration also sheds light on the academic study of "political tolerance," which gauges the willingness of citizens to uphold civil liberties for unpopular groups; and informs ongoing attempts to apply the model of toleration to contemporary debates over race, gender, sexuality, and sexual identity.

Many of toleration's defenders have sought to build upon the tolerationist accomplishments of the past, seeing them as potentially useful tools for creating societies that can manage cultural, religious, sexual, and racial differences peacefully. To many of its critics, on the contrary, toleration represents less a part of the steady advance of human freedom and more a discourse of power that continues to structure global interactions, to the detriment of marginalized and excluded populations worldwide. The contested nature of contemporary debates should not surprise us. Toleration has always been about power: who has it, who is protected by it, and on what grounds. Early modern tolerationists appealed to the state to curtail religious persecution and safeguard the rights of oppressed or disadvantaged individuals (first religious, then other types of groups). In articulating arguments against persecution and appealing to civil authorities for relief, tolerationists sought state protection for the exercise of conscience. Imperial and colonial authorities tolerated, or denied toleration, with an eye toward maintaining control and ensuring social stability. But more recent criticisms view toleration as far less liberating in nature and emphasize the ways that it can freeze in place existing social and political inequalities and enable the persistence of popular prejudice and bigotry.

Toleration, liberalism, and pluralism

Since the early modern period, toleration has become an increasingly central component of modern political thought, as both a philosophical element of the liberal creed and a substantive, if highly contested, political reality. Defenders and critics of contemporary liberalism—which identifies government's fundamental tasks as protecting individual rights, representative institutions, and market economies—have often viewed it as closely related, even virtually synonymous, with toleration. Of course, one's view of contemporary liberalism will likely shape whether one views such a close relationship as a strength or a weakness of toleration as an approach to diversity.

Those who celebrate liberal democracy and the liberal tradition, not surprisingly, frame such connections positively, and toleration appears near the top of any list of core liberal values along with liberties of speech, assembly, and press; representative institutions and constitutional government; trial by jury; and the rule of law. The preeminent liberal theorist of our time, John Rawls, viewed his "political liberalism" as the culmination of three hundred years of theorizing about the good society, rooted in the seventeenth-century struggle for religious toleration. Early modern toleration debates are of singular importance for Rawls's account of the development of contemporary liberalism: "The historical origin of political liberalism (and of liberalism more generally) is the Reformation and its aftermath, with the long controversies over religious toleration in the sixteenth and seventeenth centuries."

The importance of toleration debates for Rawls is difficult to overstate; the victory of toleration in the seventeenth century, on this view, resulted in the acceptance, not only of pluralism, but of reasonable pluralism (i.e., the presence of mutually irreconcilable, but reasonable, doctrines, both religious and non-religious). More radically, Rawls claimed that realizing his system of "justice as fairness" would "complete and extend the movement of thought that began three centuries ago with the gradual acceptance of the principle of toleration and led to... equal liberty of conscience." Similar sentiments—perhaps less grandiose, but equally substantive—have been articulated by countless liberal theorists both before and since Rawls.

But such celebrations of liberal toleration have hardly been universal. Critics have pointed to liberalism's resistance to structural critiques regarding the concentration and exercise of power, be it cultural, political, or economic; and its assimilationist demands that groups conform to liberalism's ideological parameters in exchange for inclusion in the public sphere. One of the most noteworthy such attacks during the postwar period was advanced by Robert Paul Wolff and Herbert Marcuse, in their 1965 collection *A Critique of Pure Tolerance.* (Wolff and Marcuse use the term "tolerance," though one can see from context that it does much the same work as toleration.)

In "Beyond Tolerance," the opening essay of *Critique of Pure Tolerance*, Wolff called tolerance "the virtue of the modern pluralist democracy which has emerged in contemporary

America" and traced its historical emergence to the notion that "toleration of divergent religious practices is a necessary evil" or, at best, morally neutral. However radical its roots might have been, Wolff argued, contemporary tolerance produces a public sphere biased toward the status quo, favoring established interests over marginalized or emerging groups. And despite its ostensible commitment to the rights of unpopular minorities, liberal tolerance actually offers little in the way of substantive dignity or respect, freezing inequalities in place and weakening the state's ability to promote justice and the common good. Ultimately, Wolff labeled it "indefensible in the contemporary age" and called for society to "transcend tolerance."

Marcuse's contribution to *A Critique of Pure Tolerance* took Wolff's critique a step further, arguing that "what is proclaimed and practiced as tolerance today, is in many of its most effective manifestations serving the cause of oppression." A once-radical concept has been coopted into, in Marcuse's memorable title phrase, "repressive tolerance." Focusing on widespread inequality, militarism, and class hierarchies, Marcuse warned that those pursuing truly radical paths must rediscover tolerance's partisan historical roots in opposition to majoritarian repression. Like Wolff, Marcuse implicated toleration in creating and maintaining a status quo resistant to fundamental economic and political critique, weakening progressive movements and strengthening conservative ones. Bringing the radical potential of tolerance to bear on contemporary politics would require extreme measures like "the withdrawal of toleration of speech and assembly from groups and movements which promote aggressive policies, armament, chauvinism, discrimination . . . or which oppose the extension of public services, social security, [and] medical care" and "new and rigid restrictions on teachings and practices in the educational institutions."

Such critical evaluations of tolerance in the twentieth century were provocative when first published, and they have continued to provide fodder for intense debates about the meaning and limits of toleration ever since. But the notion of a "covert" ideological dimension to toleration—muting radical critiques of the status quo, or diluting them into a tepid pluralism—is echoed by many critics who view the sort of "hands off" mentality undergirding toleration as leaving popular prejudice and bigotry intact. Although to be the object of toleration is surely to fare better, in concrete terms, than to suffer outright persecution or violence, critics often ask, might not something more ambitious be worth pursuing? Is toleration the best we can hope for?

To its critics, then, toleration is not (or not only) a noble and high-minded effort to secure just treatment for unpopular groups, but rather a privatizing and individualizing way of granting "permission" to those who nonetheless remain excluded from full membership in society. The violence and dehumanizing conditions that afflict so many in the twenty-first century is not something separable from liberal political structures, capitalistic economic relationships, and their frequent invocation of toleration as a model for social harmony, but rather integrally intertwined with them. For such critics, toleration (or tolerance) remains an inadequate and insufficient notion, an unacceptable halfway house far from the origin of modern justice a la Rawls. Rather, it yields a status well short of full citizenship and, despite its ambitious promises, represents an inadequate vehicle for pursuing true inclusion.

From religion to sexuality: culture wars and toleration

One of the most noteworthy political developments in recent years has been not only declining levels of hostility toward members of the LGBTQ community, but also an increasing acceptance of same-sex relationships and support for their public recognition, in many nations around the world. The rapid change in public attitudes over a relatively short amount of time makes this issue an especially helpful window into the contemporary politics of toleration. The widespread decriminalization of same-sex behaviors provides evidence of a minimal, but essential, baseline of legal and political protection for groups facing widespread prejudice; further measures like same-sex marriage, equal rights to adoption and inheritance, and antidiscrimination protections with regard to the workplace and commercial life provide a sense of what further degrees of inclusion might look like.

Although many religious actors have taken public stands overtly hostile to LGBTQ rights—including high-profile support for traditional sexual morality and gender roles and, more recently, efforts to secure exemptions from American antidiscrimination statutes by the Roman Catholic hierarchy and some evangelical Protestants—other commentators have drawn intriguing parallels between the historical struggles of religious and sexual minorities. While not discounting the sober assessments of toleration's practical shortcomings mentioned previously, such thinkers have insisted that the analogy to religion holds radical potential to push toward enhanced protections for sexual minorities in twenty-first-century societies. Such an explicit invocation of religion as a model, and toleration as a useful precursor, for addressing (and defusing) explosive identity-based conflicts represents one of its most important contemporary resonances and has produced vigorous arguments about the ways in which claims for religious freedom might "generalize" to other contentious aspects of identity. Just as previous generations of tolerationists pushed from the religious domain into speech, press, and free assembly, so contemporary advocates of greater inclusion for sexual minorities have attempted to build upon the historical example of religion to bolster their efforts.

The broad analogy between religion and sexuality tends to operate on the basis of a common foundation: that of ensuring citizens the opportunity to live lives of conscientious integrity in the expression of the most fundamental elements of their identities.

Such a commitment involves detaching toleration from its (historically) theistic roots and applying it to more general theories about the importance of moral conscience. Without equating conscience to sexual identity—complex and contested questions of agency and choice remain unresolved by participants in these debates—many understand struggles for inclusion on the part of sexual minorities as merely the most recent aspect of a broader historical campaign that began with religion and has expanded over the years to encompass additional dimensions of individual and group identity. An expansive understanding of conscience can thus ground protections not only for speech and press but for broader privacy rights, contraception, abortion, a variety of forms of sexual expression, and perhaps even drug use and a right to die.

If the right to the free exercise of religion is considered sacrosanct, argue such modern-day tolerationists, why is such a right not extended to other, equally foundational, aspects of individual identity? The analogy from religion to sexuality insists on individuals' right to form and, potentially, revise their understandings of their own sexual values (which encompass both bodily pleasure and morally formative relationships), as well as the opportunity to live out their sexual identities publicly. The public dimension is crucial here, as it pushes back against the individualizing and privatizing tenor of much toleration talk and leads many advocates to embrace the more expansive language of religious freedom over toleration, point toward more robust measures of inclusion, and call for a fulsome understanding of pluralism in sexual matters that makes space for competing notions of the good life in all their variety.

Political tolerance

Another way of looking more carefully at contemporary issues of inclusion and toleration involves considering the degree to which society, or its citizens, protects the basic civil rights of marginalized groups. After all, securing such protections for religious dissenters was the primary goal of early modern tolerationists. The willingness to permit things one opposes or rejects, a core practice of toleration, undergirds a whole host of such rights. Empirical research into political tolerance—generally defined as the willingness of people to support a range of civil liberties for unpopular groups, or groups toward which they feel antipathy—has long occupied political scientists and sociologists. The importance of understanding the bases of popular support for such guarantees makes political tolerance one of the central phenomena in recent political science research.

The idea of studying political tolerance emerged in the mid-twentieth-century United States, against the backdrop of the Cold War, McCarthyism, and fears of a communist conspiracy. Samuel Stouffer's *Communism, Conformity, and Civil Liberties* (1955) reported a stark set of findings: despite endorsing a wide range of civil liberties in theory, and despite ranking concerns about communism well below other issues in terms of perceived importance to their daily lives, a substantial majority of Americans remained more than willing to deny basic civil liberties to Communists. If to tolerate means to permit things of which one disapproves, Americans appeared disappointingly unwilling to do so. Decades later, the extent to which Americans supported civil liberties remained unclear. In a major 1983 report, *Dimensions of Tolerance: What Americans Believe about Civil Liberties*, Herbert McClosky and Alida Brill reported their surprise at "the frequency with which many Americans, though endorsing civil liberties in the abstract, reject them in their concrete applications." When researchers stopped providing a ready-made list of "unpopular" groups and let survey respondents choose *their own* least-favored group and then report the degree to which they would consider abridging that group's civil liberties, intolerance appeared even far more widespread, targeting a broader range of groups than had been captured by previous studies.

More recently, political tolerance research has gone global, expanding beyond its original focus on Communists to a range of other controversial groups—racists, militarists, sexual minorities, socialists, Muslims, anti-religionists, and terrorists—and exploring its manifestations beyond the American context in far-flung locales from Europe to the Global South. Changing global dynamics and events like the September 11 attacks, the War on Terror, the resurgence of Hindu nationalism in India, and U.S. President Donald Trump's advocacy of a ban on travelers from several Muslim-majority nations have clearly played an important role in shaping the prospects for political tolerance of various groups in a range of places. The 9/11 attacks, for example, revived fears of political repression akin to earlier perceptions of a Communist threat, and many have noted the analogous position occupied by twenty-first-century American Muslims when compared to mid-twentieth-century suspected Communists. Others have pointed to the potential of political intolerance to foster a culture of conformity that discourages political participation and public debate.

Although the particular groups and frameworks for understanding identity and difference have changed radically since the early modern period, the guiding question that animates concerns about political tolerance broadly parallels those that framed historical arguments over toleration: in political scientist James Gibson's words, "whether heterogeneous societies can live peacefully and democratically together." Gibson describes the dilemma of political tolerance in terms that evoke the basic picture of toleration laid out in the ancient and medieval worlds, while expanding the scope to include not merely the absence of punishment but also the right to participate in the political process:

> Tolerance means putting up with that with which one disagrees. It means allowing one's political enemies to compete openly for

> political power. A tolerant citizen is one who would not support unreasonable or discriminatory governmental restrictions on the rights of groups to participate in politics.

What constitutes "unreasonable" restrictions, as opposed to "reasonable" ones, of course, is precisely at issue in debates over political tolerance.

Toleration, empire, globalization, liberal hegemony

The issues explored above represent one aspect of recent debates over toleration: an emphasis on the internal dynamics of liberal societies and the ways that toleration can either (depending on one's politics) offer a template for addressing divisive contemporary issues or channel critique away from confronting fundamental inequalities. But political life does not neatly confine itself within national borders; toleration has long been implicated in global developments and imperial systems, and political leaders and imperial authorities employed the rhetoric of toleration to subjugate and control native populations. The identification and management of Hinduism by British authorities in India illustrated how defining beliefs and practices as "religious" represents both a means of controlling communities and a way of providing validation on the definer's terms. More recently, critics have noted the persistence of such dynamics in the context of the American Global War on Terror. Noted and controversial frameworks like Samuel Huntington's "clash of civilizations" or Bernard Lewis's claims about the decline of Islamic culture continue longer-running arguments about a liberal and tolerant "West" and non-liberal cultures and states coexisting uneasily in the global order.

Some of the most powerful critiques of toleration's role in contemporary global contexts come from those who see it as implicated in global relations of political, economic, and cultural subjugation of the Global South across a wide span of time. Christiaan Snouck Hurgronje, an early twentieth-century Dutch colonial advisor in Indonesia, divided Islam divided into a "religion" and a "political doctrine," and used such a division to propose toleration of Islam as a religion but ruthless suppression of anything resembling an Islamic political movement. More recently, the propensity of Western elites to essentialize complex entities like Islam can make it impossible to understand the concrete and contingent political factors that drive much international conflict. So long as Western elites view the Islamist "threat" as driven primarily by an intolerant and fundamentalist strand of Islam, concrete aggravating factors like U.S. support for Israel, which galvanizes animosity toward the United States among many of the world's Muslims, are rendered invisible. (The outbreak of violence on and after the October 2023 Hamas attacks on Israel has brought these issues to the fore once again, in tragic and bloody ways.)

The widespread Western bifurcation between "good Muslims" and "bad Muslims"—in which good Muslims receive toleration and bad Muslims face the full force of Western military power—provides a foundation for an understanding of global religious freedom pitting representatives of "good" (i.e., liberal, peaceful, amenable to "Western" values) religion, who are deemed deserving of toleration and support, against "bad religions," which are designated as an existential threat and face eradication by Western counterterrorism operatives.

Toleration and "negative liberty"

With the unprecedented global movement of people, be it voluntary migration or refugees fleeing war, privation, oppression, or climate change-induced hardship, contemporary societies face increasing levels and types of diversity. Such developments, and the demographic and cultural transformations that have gone along with them, have prompted intense debate about the acceptable extent, permissible limits, and conceptual foundations of toleration, as well as its relationship to questions of multiculturalism and "identity" politics. Whether we are speaking of narrowly religious issues or broader social categories, the phenomenon of toleration—in its classic form, as it pertains to marginalized religious groups, or in the guise of "political tolerance," or even invoked as simply "tolerance"—retains a vital contemporary importance.

Although longstanding historical connections exist between toleration and the liberal democratic tradition, assuming that those connections are somehow essential—that, for example, toleration is the exclusive possession of liberal democratic constitutional regimes, or of the "Western political tradition"—obscures our capacity to see the ways in which societies with different cultural and political traditions can create protections for the marginalized groups in their midst.

Much of the discontent with toleration as an ideal among its contemporary critics has to do with the negative, or at least partial, degree to which it addresses questions of inclusion and social acceptance. These aspects of toleration are, to some extent, built into the idea itself, insofar as an "objection component" constitutes a central part of its conceptual structure. Early modern tolerationists, after all, sought first and foremost to end persecution and ensure that members of dissenting religious communities would not be punished for exercising the liberty of their consciences. In this sense, toleration is at root a "negative liberty": although the term has evolved to include positive elements undreamt of by earlier generations (receipt of public benefits in modern welfare states, for example), toleration leans heavily on the cessation of punishment at its core. This claim about toleration prioritizing freedom from punishment does not preclude protracted arguments over precisely what constitutes such freedom today, as opposed to the sixteenth century, and we should not expect that our definitions will exactly match early modern ones. Still, critics of "mere" toleration have perennially (and accurately) pointed out that it makes few demands in terms of attitudinal tolerance or equal respect, and that it frequently perpetuates systems in which tolerators get to decide who receives toleration and who does not.

At the same time, the negative liberty at the heart of toleration is no static phenomenon, and it has proven itself to be a protean and elastic concept. There is a world of difference, of course, between baseline toleration toward LGBTQ individuals and more robust measures of inclusion such as same-sex marriage and equal protection guaranteed by antidiscrimination statutes. Yet the latter is unthinkable without the prior achievement of the former. A similar point applies to the more traditional domain of religion. The Toleration Act in England, hailed by many as a milestone of early modern toleration, allowed a number of restrictive practices to remain in place; the story of successive generations of religious minorities in England is the story of gradual and hard-fought efforts to repeal restrictions on their fuller incorporation into English public life. Such efforts are not "complete" today, to be sure, and inclusion remains, for many, a continuing struggle.

Similarly, reifying "toleration" into a discrete set of conditions that, once met, ends political debate—a box to be checked, so to speak—fails to do justice to the ongoing quest for liberty of conscience in its many forms. Proponents of liberty of conscience historically sought a steadily expanding sphere in which religious concerns were removed as bases for punishment, persecution, or the denial of civic membership. The nature and contours of that expansion, however, represent a series of specific and local applications achieved only after protracted political struggles. In the difficult historical emergence of toleration, we encounter painful compromises, hard-headed political negotiations, and a search for political and legal measures to ensure equal citizenship regardless of individuals' beliefs, practices, or identities. Toleration, then, may best be understood as an ongoing process, never complete, always a matter of struggle, and never assured of success. The violent and bloody history of the twentieth century provides all the evidence needed to drive home the precarity of toleration as a political accomplishment. Far from having moved "beyond toleration," as George Washington so confidently proclaimed to the Hebrew Congregation in Newport more than two centuries ago, questions of toleration remain an ever-present site of political contestation well into the twenty-first century.

Chapter 7
The future of toleration?

The emergence and development of toleration forms part of a larger story of political struggle, initially in the realm of religion and gradually expanding to debates over civil liberties, sexuality, cultural diversity, and global conflict. The types of issues that animate contemporary questions of religious freedom may seem light years away from the early modern debates between Protestants and Catholics (and, often, between groups of rival Protestants) that gave rise to such foundational achievements as the 1689 Toleration Act. Issues like Rastafarian prisoners suing American prison authorities for violating their religious freedom by shaving their dreadlocks, or the charges (and countercharges) of antisemitism and Islamophobia that took on new urgency in the wake of the October 7 Hamas attacks on Israel and the ensuing Israeli military operations in Gaza, illustrate just how difficult it is to neatly separate categories like "religion" and "politics" in the contemporary political world.

What about the future? Is toleration in fact, as many of its critics have charged, an outdated, outmoded, inadequate, and unhelpful concept for dealing with twenty-first-century realities? Or might it retain some importance, even in radically different circumstances than those of its early modern emergence? Considering one of the best-known twentieth-century frameworks for analyzing tolerance and intolerance can provide a window into some widespread assumptions about the politics of tolerance in contemporary societies.

Although Karl Popper's "paradox of tolerance" originally appeared in a footnote, as part of a critique of Plato's *Republic* within a much longer work, it has become a widely known way of framing the dilemmas that toleration poses in today's world, particularly with regard to the presence of "intolerant" groups within larger societies. In his classic 1945 study, *The Open Society and Its Enemies*, Popper introduced his "paradox of tolerance," which in its most straightforward formulation claims that "unlimited tolerance must lead to the disappearance of tolerance." He continues, "If we extend unlimited tolerance even to those who are intolerant, if we are not prepared to defend a tolerant society against the onslaught of the intolerant, then the tolerant will be destroyed, and tolerance with them." In other words, those who embrace unlimited tolerance ultimately ensure their own destruction. Society is under no obligation to tolerate the intolerant; indeed, to do so represents a step toward collective suicide. Popper explains:

> If we extend unlimited tolerance even to those who are intolerant, if we are not prepared to defend a tolerant society against the onslaught of the intolerant, then the tolerant will be destroyed, and tolerance with them.... I do not imply...that we should always suppress the utterance of intolerant philosophies; as long as we can counter them by rational argument and keep them in check by public opinion, suppression would certainly be most unwise. But we should claim the right to suppress them if necessary even by force; for it may easily turn out that they are not prepared to meet us on the level of rational argument, but begin by denouncing all argument; they may forbid their followers to listen to rational argument, because it is deceptive, and teach them to answer arguments by the use of their fists or pistols. We should therefore claim, in the name of tolerance, the right not to tolerate the intolerant.

One important piece of historical context here: the rise of Hitler and the Nazi party shaped Popper's analysis in fundamental ways. "The final decision to write [*The Open Society and Its Enemies*] was made in March 1938," he wrote, "on the day I received the news of the invasion of Austria," and he described the book's goal as "an attempt to understand those events and their background, and some of the issues which were likely to arise after the war was won." Hence the twin phenomena of Nazism and Marxism as social movements loomed large for Popper; Nazi Germany and the Soviet Union served as exemplars of closed societies, which he contrasted with open societies in which individuals exercise "rational personal responsibility" over their life choices.

But no theorist of toleration has ever argued for unlimited tolerance, nor is it even clear what such a term might mean. What Popper is describing here—"unlimited tolerance"—is not only a straw position, but an argument bordering on the disingenuous. Thinkers and political actors in the tolerationist tradition have always articulated the limits of toleration as an integral part of their defenses of it.

Such limits have shifted over time, for different reasons and shaped by different contexts, but always as part of a political process. The notion of "public safety," "social order," or the "national interest" as a limit to toleration has long functioned as a way of offering legal protections to some forms of belief and behavior while justifying restrictions on others. (Whether governments use such justifications sincerely, or as a smokescreen to silence opposition, is a different question.) President George Washington expressed to the 1789 Quaker Yearly Meeting his desire "that the laws may always be as extensively accommodated to them, as a due regard to the protection and essential interests of the nation may justify and permit." It is a striking sentence, shadowed by Washington's distrust of the pacifist Quakers, whom he perceived as having been less than supportive of the American side during the Revolution. Washington proclaimed the importance of treating Quakers' conscientious scruples, which included refusing to bear arms and swear oaths, with delicacy and tenderness, while reiterating that this grant of liberty was subject to limitation based on the "essential interest of the nation." Likewise, Mill's harm principle offered a conceptually clear, if practically murky, limit—harm to others—as an indication of the outer limits of toleration. In our own time, even the most expansive human rights documents generally include some mention of public order or safety as a legitimate justification for curtailing the toleration of dissent.

So the premise of Popper's formulation, this purported embrace of "unlimited tolerance," turns out, upon closer examination, to be a mirage. More problematically, however, Popper populates his political landscape with two discrete and easily discernible camps: the tolerant on the one hand, and the intolerant on the other. It is, to say the least, a radically oversimplified picture of the complex nature of political life. The tolerant (to whom Popper consistently refers as "we") play an entirely defensive role, seeking only to defend open societies. The intolerant, by contrast, are active and undermining in nature; they engage in an "onslaught" against free society, attempting to get their way by using "fists or pistols." Against such a foe, who could deny that those defending tolerance have both the moral high ground and the absolute right to defeat the intolerant by any means necessary, to place them, in Popper's words, "outside the law" and treat them as "criminal"? (As he put it, "We should claim the right to suppress them if necessary even by force.") Labeling one's opponents as "intolerant" offers an easy way to discredit their ideas and practices, cast them as a political threat, and facilitate turning the full force of coercive state power on them.

This observation is by no means intended to understate or minimize the horrors of Nazi Germany, which shaped Popper's vision of what a prototypical "intolerant" party looked like, and what the consequences of tolerating such a group were likely to be.

The tolerance of intolerance, as he understood it, yielded genocide, world war, and death camps. Yet despite Popper's clean dichotomy, the tolerant and the intolerant are not free-floating categories, clearly distinguishable by objective criteria. Rather, labeling political actors as tolerant or intolerant is itself a political act. Early modern tolerationists sought to redefine prevailing political understandings of religious dissent away from association with sedition and disloyalty and, conversely, to assert its fundamental compatibility with political society. Fundamental to that political process were frequent attempts to present their rivals—be they Roman Catholics or Protestant antitolerationists—as politically unsound, intolerant, and destabilizing. Religious dissenters often appealed to the state for protection against ecclesiastical actors like established churches, appealing to state authorities who were themselves looking to consolidate their power and establish sovereignty over their territories.

Notwithstanding its widespread popularity and the myriad horrors associated with twentieth-century Nazi and Communist totalitarianisms, Popper's paradox threatens to stifle political debate in profound ways. His rhetorical dichotomy between "rational argument" and "pistols and fists" shows how contemporary advocates of toleration often frame themselves as reasonable defenders of civilized society, the only thing standing between civilization and barbarism, while painting their opponents as violent extremists worthy of suppression or exclusion.

Although Popper's formulation has proven to be controversial, he is hardly alone in his central contention. Scholars studying political tolerance often evoke similar sentiments, as when political scientist Paul Sniderman and colleagues differentiate between groups with different ideas and those who undertake violent or illegal conduct: "To refuse to tolerate socialists is to be intolerant; but to refuse to tolerate terrorists is to be tolerant."

In our own time, rhetoric about a "clash of civilizations" and the inherently intolerant or antidemocratic character of Islam often serves as a pretext for surveillance, exclusion, and violence against Muslims in the United States and Europe (and beyond). The widespread targeting of Muslims, and their portrayal in the media as a group outside the realm of the tolerable, presents them as inherently politically dangerous and problematic for liberal democracy, beyond the bounds of toleration. The increasing prominence of securitization rhetoric, which transforms policy disputes into national or global security issues, frequently justifies incursions on civil liberties in response to such purported threats.

It should come as no surprise that toleration has always been a partisan notion as well as a relational one, deployed by groups against other groups or their governments (or both). There is no abstract question of toleration, after all; such disputes are always particular ones, involving a series of concrete questions. Toleration for whom? On what grounds? Toward what end? Under what conditions? With what limits? Granted by what authority? The struggle for toleration represents one part of broader struggles for acceptance, recognition, inclusion, and power: not the culmination of the struggle, but the establishment of a basic level of legal and political security, a prelude to further theorizing and mobilization. Necessary, we might say, while not necessarily sufficient. But we need something much more nuanced than Popper's approach to understand the dynamics most likely to provide supportive contexts for the emergence of toleration in our own times.

Outmoded? Outdated? Irrelevant?

If the rise of Nazism provided the context for Popper's paradox, the postwar period saw attempts at codifying human rights and building a global consensus about, among other things, religious freedom and liberty of conscience. In December 1948 the United Nations General Assembly proclaimed the Universal Declaration of Human Rights. Article 18 of the UDHR set out liberty of conscience as a fundamental human right:

> Everyone has the right to freedom of thought, conscience and religion [including] freedom to change his religion or belief, and freedom, either alone or in community with others and in public or private, to manifest his religion or belief in teaching, practice, worship and observance.

Similar wording appears in other international agreements and declarations, including Articles 18 and 27 of the International Covenant on Civil and Political Rights (1966) and Articles 1 and 6 of the Declaration on the Elimination of All Forms of Intolerance and of Discrimination Based on Religion or Belief (1981).

In keeping with efforts to embrace more capacious notions of human dignity, these documents tend to eschew the language of toleration, substituting that of rights, freedom, or equality. The UDHR, for example, speaks in terms of rights, and the Declaration aims to eradicate "intolerance," but says little about its inverse, with the exception of calling for "understanding, tolerance and respect in matters relating to freedom of religion or belief." American diplomacy, too, employs this distinction between tolerance and freedom. The U.S. Commission on International Religious Freedom distinguishes between "religious tolerance" and "freedom of religion and belief," presenting the latter as its standard for judging the actions of nations around the globe. According to the Commission (in a declaration that, to put it mildly, reflects geopolitical dynamics and concerns), "Authoritarian states promote religious tolerance, without necessarily ensuring freedom of religion or belief."

Such a distinction is also part of academic commentary on these global developments. The lead editor of a mammoth resource published by the Oslo Coalition on Freedom of Religion or Belief—a 1,000-page "Deskbook" that originated in a conference to celebrate the UDHR's fiftieth anniversary—refers to toleration as a "half-hearted expedient" that falls well short of trust or mutual respect and offers only "a merely prudential determination to put up with other beliefs." Toleration does nothing, in other words, to foster our capacities to engage, respect, and understand the different ideas and practices of other groups with whom we share our community. For many human rights advocates, something much more substantive is needed to realize the promise of coexistence in conditions of deep diversity.

This movement away from toleration as a guiding metaphor parallels an expansion in the phenomena being protected, which are no longer restricted to "religion" narrowly defined. Freedom of "thought, conscience, and religion" (UDHR) or "religion and belief" (Declaration) includes the religious grounds that formed such an important part of toleration's history but opens outward toward more general foundations of individual and group identity. In this sense, the expansive potential of toleration continues to develop: from protecting narrowly religious phenomena to acknowledging the more general moral and philosophical commitments that provide contemporary individuals with resources for solidarity and group membership.

For many observers, the choice to use the language of freedom over that of toleration is indicative of unease around toleration's checkered history and minimalist nature, and of a desire for more fulsome responses to diversity and inequality. Representatives from various religious and ethical traditions have offered formulas for interreligious dialogue and reconciliation that see the value of tolerance and toleration (if at all) primarily as a means to other ends, needing eventually to give way to respect, humility, and substantive engagement. (Some draw explicitly on Gandhi.) In addition, an East Asian, Taoist-influenced view takes issue with the entire notion of "objection" at the heart of toleration, calling instead for modeling positive respect and an embrace of other ways of life. A common thread links these critiques: mere toleration, or tolerance, is decidedly inferior to a robust ethical stance that seeks to benefit (and not merely refrain from interfering with) others whose ways of life may be different from one's own.

Nonetheless, in broader public commentary and analysis of public affairs, "tolerance" often retains a prominent place, as evidenced by its frequent invocation by political elites as a way of describing their aspirations for contemporary multicultural societies. The Mission Statement of the Penn Biden Center for Diplomacy and Global Engagement beckons to "a democratic, open, secure, tolerant, and interconnected world benefits all Americans." And at a 2017 ceremony marking the 500th anniversary of the Reformation, German Chancellor Angela Merkel voiced her conviction that "whoever believes in diversity must also practice tolerance," which she called "the basis for peaceful co-existence in Europe." (She has also referred to tolerance as "the soul of Europe.")

Many observers rightly push back against such claims, and the historical record—in Europe as well as elsewhere—does not necessarily lend itself to such definitive praise. But tolerance also frequently appears in educational contexts, dedicated to teaching strategies for coexistence and encouraging the peaceful settlement of differences; as a more general educational aim of fostering "deliberative virtues" among those with differing cultural, ethnic, racial, or religious backgrounds; and as a way of addressing the appeal of extremism and radicalism to young people and building dialogue across religious and other boundaries. Historical and philosophical drawbacks notwithstanding, tolerance and toleration retain their aspirational appeal for many.

Ultimately, one of the important issues that will shape the future of toleration, and its capacity to inform ongoing issues of theory and practice, is the increasing instability and lack of consensus about the very idea of "religion" itself. The early modern context in which toleration rose to conceptual and political prominence focused not only on beliefs but also on practice, ritual, public worship, assembly, and speech. That said, many tolerationists emphasized the inner or inward aspect of religion (Locke's "inward persuasion of the mind"). As a result, much of the literature on toleration has emphasized conflict over belief and proceeded as if the main challenge, politically speaking, was securing the liberty to believe as one was persuaded, to follow the dictates of belief as they manifested themselves in various aspects of individual and group life. The legal and political terrain on which toleration is fought out is more complex now than it has ever been. American courts often seem unable to clearly identity the phenomenon in question when ruling on matters of religion, and the intertwined nature of caste, culture, ethnicity, and race raised in many pressing global conflicts calls into question the idea of religion as a clearly bounded entity, neatly separable from other aspects of individual or group identity.

Minimal, incomplete, but worth preserving

Even if we take toleration to be partial, minimalistic, and ultimately insufficient as a measure of full inclusion, as some of its critics suggest, such a dismissal runs the risk of throwing out the proverbial baby with the bathwater. Intolerance and persecution continue to be everyday realities for members of religious, ethnic, or other minoritized groups in advanced democracies as well as authoritarian countries. Toleration does not offer a panacea for such groups—it did not in the early modern period, and it certainly does not now—but it can offer a language for giving voice to their experiences and expressing their aspirations to live lives of conscientious integrity. The vocabulary of toleration can offer a conceptual shape and historical pedigree to proposals for concrete improvements in the everyday experiences of many of these groups. A non-exhaustive list, to say the least:

- Muslims in India have faced discrimination and violence for decades and particularly in recent years with the resurgence of Hindu nationalism under the government of Prime Minister Narendra Modi. Discrimination and coercion can operate in subtler ways as well, as in the case of India's cow protection legislation that many (including the U.S. State Department) interpret as thinly veiled religious intolerance.
- Across South Asia more broadly, culturally hegemonic religions (Islam in Pakistan, Buddhism in Sri Lanka and Myanmar) pose challenges to the ability of religious and cultural minorities to retain their distinctive customs and rituals and to structure their lives accordingly.
- LGBTQ individuals continue to experience hostility and violence worldwide. The 2023 Ugandan law that made homosexuality a capital offense represents the most extreme example, but discrimination and exclusion persist around the world. The U.S. Supreme Court has ruled in favor of evangelical Christians who consider antidiscrimination laws designed to protect LGBTQ individuals to be violations of their religious freedom. Such exclusion is largely economic—involving refusals to provide goods and services for same-sex couples—but the disputes raise questions about inclusion more generally, and about the connection between such hostility and the commission of hate crimes against LGBTQ Americans.
- Communities such as the Rohingya and Uyghurs, in which the grounds for marginalization include both religious and ethnic dimensions, have faced persecution and genocidal violence from the governments of China and Myanmar. They continue to suffer even in the presence of a worldwide outcry against the conditions to which they are subjected.
- Conflicts between colonial authorities and indigenous groups have often manifested themselves in the arena of religious practice and

ritual. The Native American Church's rituals involving peyote use collided with American drug laws and led to the Supreme Court's 1990 *Smith* decision upholding restrictions on the drug's usage, while the passage of the Religious Freedom Restoration Act of 1993 aimed to set a high bar for any infringement on American religious exercise. But related issues, such as those involving destruction of sacred lands and the horrific history of Native boarding schools, which attempted to extinguish all trace of indigenous culture in the name of "civilizing" Native children, are not always best served by the individualistic nature of documents like the UDHR. The 2007 UN Declaration of the Rights of Indigenous Peoples (particularly Article 12) designated "peoples" as rights holders and offered the possibility of a more appropriate understanding of indigenous spiritualities. Still, the legal landscape for indigenous activism remains daunting.

- The French headscarf debate and related controversies (such as proposed burkini bans) have long implicated French views of Islam, the legacy of French colonialism, and the exclusionary nature of French secularism (*laicité*). Yet there has also been a great deal of debate about just how to characterize the head coverings at the heart of this issue, and whether calling them "Islamic" or even "religious" does justice to the varied reasons that women might have for wearing them. (The headscarf issue is hardly limited to France; it has occasioned debates in other European nations including Turkey, and the United States as well.)
- Beyond the debates over articles of clothing, conflicts over space have also served to highlight U.S. and European attitudes toward Islam. In some European contexts minarets have been banned even where Christian church spires remain permitted, and some American localities have sought to prevent the construction of mosques by manipulating zoning regulations.

These cases, along with the actions of the U.S. State Department and the Commission on International Religious Freedom, remind us that toleration always comes enmeshed in relations of power.

The global power exercised by the United States makes its annual Report on International Religious Freedom more than a mere recitation of facts about policies; it is itself an exercise of political power. Naming certain practices "violations" and certain countries as "violators" can serve as a prelude to designating them "Countries of Particular Concern" that countenance "particularly severe violations of religious freedom"; or, slightly less drastically, placement on a State Department "Special Watch List." Even non-state actors like the Wagner Group or Boko Haram face assignment as "Entities of Particular Concern." American foreign policy and Western powers more generally thus promote a distinction between good and bad religion, with tolerant religion in the former category and countries and movements hostile to American interests labeled as "bad" and targeted as dangerous threats to civilized order. (Nor is this an entirely new development, as the U.S. role in imposing its notion of religious freedom on Japan after World War II demonstrates.) Without commenting on the specifics of any case, it is worth noting how the list of such countries and entities overlaps with American alliances and rivalries worldwide.

Reconsidering the *modus vivendi* regime

Given their historical placement and the concrete and violent realities of the times in which they lived, most early modern tolerationists sought a realistic and sustainable way of living together that avoided the predictable worst-case scenarios of violent discord and intercommunal violence. Such a goal did not promise a resolution of all differences (religious or otherwise) but offered concrete benefits for both tolerator and tolerated. One of the great legacies of early modern toleration for the history of liberal thought and practice lies in the recognition that (as John Rawls would later put it) societies were now, and would continue to be, characterized not simply by pluralism, but by "reasonable pluralism."

So tolerationist policies sought something rather minimal at the outset: the creation of a public space in which individuals and groups of differing persuasions could live out their own conceptions of truth and the demands it placed on their lives. Toleration has long appealed to participants in such debates, insofar as it valorized the voluntary affirmation of commitments that flow from individuals' deepest ethical, moral, or religious beliefs. The early modern details may seem minimal—indeed, they are minimal—when compared with twentieth-century notions of equal concern and respect, and the celebration of difference. But we should not be so hasty to dismiss the value of what has come to be called a *modus vivendi*, and the basic toleration that historically accompanied it, and we should appreciate how effective such minimal agreements can be (and, historically, have been) in protecting basic rights and providing a foundation for further mobilization and advocacy. Early modern achievements were never static ones. Tolerationist thinkers built on an expansive notion of conscience and its prerogatives, of liberty of conscience as encompassing not only freedom of individual belief but also of corporate religious exercise, and a broad resistance to civil liabilities for religious non-conformity. And later actors built on the work of earlier ones.

A *modus vivendi* tolerationist state, like any state, is an imperfect vessel. It does not offer blanket declarations of state neutrality or respect for all citizens' views of the good, but instead attempts to promote a pacific public space in which citizens can live out their deepest commitments. Understood this way, the achievement of basic toleration ends one process and begins another, offering an opportunity to carve out basic protections and to seek a position from which to pursue more capacious notions of what a society that respects human dignity and conscientious integrity might look like. Given that contemporary societies are characterized by seemingly intractable divisions on religious, moral, and philosophical views, some citizens will continue to view the practices of others not merely with suspicion or ignorance, but with well-informed hatred. *Modus vivendi* tolerationism offers a chastened politics, committed to seeking coexistence even while realizing that fundamentally conflicting values are part of the permanent human landscape.

Toleration is no panacea for social difference, economic inequality, political exclusion, and popular prejudice. But neither should we expect our political concepts to perform impossible tasks. Toleration has proven most effective, historically speaking, in framing a particular type of difference and articulating the vital importance of individuals and groups living lives of conscientious integrity. Toleration is not entirely distinct from more expansive notions of liberty, equality, inclusion, and the like, and many of the same aspirations that fired mobilization against overt persecution can facilitate further thinking about what those notions might look like in new and different circumstances. A firm commitment to equal protection of the law, equal opportunity, and a structure of basic civil rights might indeed seem minimal against the background of calls for the celebration of difference and equal respect. But if toleration is ultimately necessary, but not sufficient, for such equal respect, there continue to be large areas of the globe where the basic protection of fundamental rights remain insecure. The precarious nature of such populations, even in advanced democracies, suggests that the tolerationist legacy will remain vitally relevant.

Further reading

Adcock, Cassie S. *The Limits of Tolerance: Indian Secularism and the Politics of Religious Freedom*. Oxford and New York: Oxford University Press, 2014.

Asoka. *Edicts of Asoka*. Translated by G. Srinivasa Murti and A. N. Krishna Aiyangar. Madras: Adyar Library, 1951.

Bejan, Teresa M. *Mere Civility: Disagreement and the Limits of Toleration*. Cambridge, MA: Harvard University Press, 2017.

Beneke, Chris. *Beyond Toleration: The Religious Origins of American Pluralism*. New York: Oxford University Press, 2006.

Brown, Wendy. *Regulating Aversion: Tolerance in the Age of Identity and Empire*. Princeton, NJ: Princeton University Press, 2008.

Cohen, Andrew Jason. *Toleration and Freedom from Harm: Liberalism Reconceived*. New York: Routledge, 2018.

de Roover, Jakob. *Europe, India, and the Limits of Secularism*. New Delhi: Oxford University Press, 2015.

Finkel, Irving L., ed. *The Cyrus Cylinder: The King of Persia's Proclamation from Ancient Babylon*. London: I. B. Tauris, 2013.

Forst, Rainer. *Toleration in Conflict: Past and Present*. Cambridge: Cambridge University Press, 2013.

Gaustad, Edwin S. *Roger Williams*. New York: Oxford University Press, 2005.

Haefeli, Evan. *Accidental Pluralism: America and the Religious Politics of English Expansion, 1497–1662*. Chicago: University of Chicago Press, 2021.

Jakobsen, Janet R., and Ann Pellegrini. *Love the Sin: Sexual Regulation and the Limits of Religious Tolerance*. New York: New York University Press, 2003.

Kamen, Henry. *Spain's Road to Empire: The Making of a World Power; 1492–1763*. London: Penguin, 2002.

King, Preston. *Toleration*. New York: St. Martin's Press, 1976.

Lahiri, Nayanjot. *Ashoka in Ancient India*. Cambridge, MA: Harvard University Press, 2015.

Laursen, John Christian, ed. *Religious Toleration: "The Variety of Rites" from Cyrus to Defoe*. New York: St. Martin's Press, 1999.

Lecler, Joseph. *Toleration and the Reformation*. 2 vols. New York: Association Press, 1960.

MacCulloch, Diarmaid. *The Reformation*. New York: Viking, 2004.

McNally, Michael David. *Defend the Sacred: Native American Religious Freedom beyond the First Amendment*. Princeton, NJ: Princeton University Press, 2020.

Mendus, Susan, ed. *Justifying Toleration: Conceptual and Historical Perspectives*. Cambridge: Cambridge University Press, 1988.

Menocal, Maria Rosa. *The Ornament of the World: How Muslims, Jews, and Christians Created a Culture of Tolerance in Medieval Spain*. Boston: Little, Brown, 2002.

Moore, Robert I. *The Formation of a Persecuting Society: Authority and Deviance in Western Europe, 950–1250*. 2nd ed. Malden, MA: Blackwell, 2007.

Murphy, Andrew R. *William Penn: A Life*. New York: Oxford University Press, 2019.

Nederman, Cary J., and John Christian Laursen, eds. *Difference and Dissent: Theories of Toleration in Medieval and Early Modern Europe*. Lanham, MD: Rowman & Littlefield, 1996.

Nirenberg, David. *Communities of Violence: Persecution of Minorities in the Middle Ages*. Princeton, NJ: Princeton University Press, 1996.

Popper, Karl R. *The Open Society and Its Enemies*. Princeton, NJ: Princeton University Press, 2013.

Rawls, John. *Political Liberalism*. New York: Columbia University Press, 1993.

Richards, David A. J. *Identity and the Case for Gay Rights: Race, Gender, Religion as Analogies*. Chicago: University of Chicago Press, 1999.

Schwartz, Stuart B. *All Can Be Saved: Religious Tolerance and Salvation in the Iberian Atlantic World*. New Haven, CT: Yale University Press, 2008.

Smith, Vincent A. *Akbar the Great Mogul, 1542–1605*. Oxford: Clarendon Press, 1917.

Sorkin, David Jan. *Jewish Emancipation: A History Across Five Centuries*. Princeton, NJ: Princeton University Press, 2019.

Stepan, Alfred C., ed. *Boundaries of Toleration*. New York: Columbia University Press, 2014.

Waters, Matthew W. *King of the World: The Life of Cyrus the Great*. New York: Oxford University Press, 2022.

Wilken, Robert Louis. *Liberty in the Things of God: The Christian Origins of Religious Freedom*. New Haven, CT: Yale University Press, 2019.

Wolff, Robert Paul, Barrington Moore Jr., and Herbert Marcuse. *A Critique of Pure Tolerance*. Boston: Beacon, 1969.

Index

Note: Figures are indicated by an italic "*f*" following the page number.

For the benefit of digital users, indexed terms that span two pages (e.g., 52–53) may, on occasion, appear on only one of those pages.

A

B

J

K

L

M

Q

R

U

W